THE
320
LIFE

The Life You Always Wanted
and Wondered How to Have

Wendy Pope

Author of Best-Seller *Wait and See:*
Finding Peace in God's Pauses and Plans

To the Ladies of the Hillcrest Women's Conference of 2021

Count your chicken nuggets every time.

Contents

WEEK 4

Welcome to Bible Study

I love Bible study! And I really LOVE studying the Bible with friends. We need Bible Study, and we also need community. But our lives are so busy that we don't always have time to show up in person each week, on the right day (not that I have *ever* shown up on the wrong day), kids in tow, answers completed, ready to sit still for an hour and a half. For this reason, I appreciate the beauty and ease of online studies. You are able to watch the teachings and finish your study questions when your schedule allows . . . and you never have to pack a kid in the car.

That's one of the reasons I put this Bible study together. I'm thrilled to commemorate the literary birthday of my second book, *Yes, No, and Maybe: Living with the God of Immeasurably More*, by releasing her cousin, *The 320 Life: The Life You Always Wanted and Wondered How to Have*, complete with free online teachings for you. Simply scan this QR code to access the accompanying video teachings on my website.

If you've read *Yes, No, and Maybe*, no worries! The Bible study material in this book is brand new; I've never published or taught it in an online format. The Word of God is alive and active and is always teaching us. With the Holy Spirit's help, we have all new Bible Study content here. Hallelujah and amen!

We will spend the next four weeks studying the 320 Life, digging deep into God's Word. Each week will be filled with relevant, uplifting devotions and:

- ❖ Something to Pursue: Challenge verse
  A Bible verse to study and learn

- ❖ Something to Hold Onto: Immeasurably More statement to anchor your thoughts
  A rhythmic statement to help you grab hold of the week's main topic

- ❖ Something to View: Video teaching
  A video listening guide to follow as you watch the video teaching

- ❖ Something to Do: Bible study questions
  Personal reflection and questions to deepen your study

❖ Something to Renew You: Just between you and Jesus journal pages
A place to write what you hear from the Lord

In our four-week study, we will clearly define the 320 Life and deeply study the God who is able to do immeasurably more than we can ask or imagine. This life is discovered by living three spiritual principles:

❖ *Yes* cultivates trust *in* God

❖ *No* invites revelation *from* God

❖ *Maybe* welcomes freedom *with* God

In addition to these 320 Life principles, we will be highlighting the apostle Paul and four powerful passages from Psalm 119, the longest chapter in the Bible. The authors, who scholars suggest are David, Ezra, Daniel, and Moses, address the difficulties of life through the power of God's Word. The four passages from Psalm 119 will also be our weekly challenge verses. I encourage you to read the entire psalm, all 176 verses— multiple times and, if possible, out loud. *(Helpful hint: break up the chapter into bite size pieces to help you read the whole thing.)* God's Word, and our obedience to its truths, is the conduit to the life you've always wanted and wondered how to have.

Grab your Bible, some highlighters (you're going to need them), and your favorite pen. Since the class is online, the schedule is flexible. You can view the teachings when it works best for you; if you are meeting with a group, you can get together any time.

Our precious and patient Lord taught me these three spiritual principles of yes, no, and maybe almost two decades ago, and I still live by them today. It is through them that I have cultivated a confident faith and now live fully in the freedom Jesus died to give me. It gives me such great joy to take this journey with you. Oh, it must delight our Heavenly Father, Savior, and the Holy Spirit to know that we are investing so much time in studying His magnificent and powerful Word.

Let's get this party started,

Wendy

P.S. In case you miss a blank on the Listening Guides during the teaching, the answers are provided in the back.

Week 1

THE WEALTH
OF THE 320 LIFE

The life you always wanted to live
begins with *yes* to God.

Devotion

ACCEPTING FORGIVENESS

"What happiness for those whose guilt has been forgiven! What joys when sins are covered over! What relief for those who have confessed their sins and God has cleared their record." Ps. 32:1–2 (TLB)

Women following Christ are supposed to allow God's truth to define who they are. *But do we?* On good days, yes: when the sky is clear blue, when our ducks are in a row, and when our quiet time is on point. *Then* we believe God's definition of who we are.

But what about the other days when none of that happens? What about when we go weeks without reading our Bible, when we yell horrible things at our children, or when we sin to the point that we are too ashamed to admit it to God? What defines us then?

For years, I defined myself by my previous sins and failures. The regret over my sins from my past weighed heavy on my heart and mind. I had hurt others and myself. I replayed my decisions and cringe over my failures. Two decades later, the grip of old sins still had a hold on me. And don't get me started on the day-to-day failings that racked me with guilt.

I confessed my past sins to God and asked Him to pardon me. I consistently sought His forgiveness for my current sins. Yet, even though I knew that He'd forgiven me, I couldn't accept the freedom of His forgiveness. I wanted so badly to believe I was the person David mentions in Psalm 32:2, "What relief for those who have confessed their sins and God has cleared their record" (TLB). But I struggled to accept that God's grace could erase my sins—wiping them away as if they'd never happened—and abolish my guilt.

We all sin, but we are not our sin—even when the enemy tries to convince us to define ourselves by what we have done. This can be a hard thing to accept for many of us. It sounds all well and good, but, in reality, the weight, memory, and consequences of sin make it difficult for us to believe that a perfect God can forgive and not count our sin against us. But God's Word assures us of that. So how can we live in this truth?

The first step is to believe that Christ died for the forgiveness of our sin: "God made him who had no sin to be sin for us, so that in him we might become the righteousness of God" (2 Cor. 5:21 [NIV]).

The second step is to acknowledge our sin—to ourselves and to God. This opens up the door for honest conversations with the Lord and helps us to stop hiding from the fear of being found out.

The next step is to fill our hearts and minds with truth. Throughout the Bible, God teaches how an unaccepting heart can be changed and softened to accept His forgiveness. The following verses are truth from a loving God who longs to transform our lives through the grace of His forgiveness.

> **My master is grace, not sin.**
> "Sin is no longer your master, for you no longer live under the requirements of the law. Instead, you live under the freedom of God's grace." Rom. 6:14 (NLT)

> **My Savior Jesus has set me free, therefore I am free.**
> "So if the Son sets you free, you will be free indeed." John 8:36 (NIV)

> **My old is gone; because of Jesus Christ, I am forgiven.**
> "If we confess our sins, he is faithful and just to forgive us our sins and to cleanse us from all unrighteousness." 1 John 1:9 (ESV)

If you are lugging around a load of sin that God has already forgiven, re-read the verses above and thank God for His freedom and forgiveness. Are you ready to stop living in shame, defined by your past? Pray and ask God to redirect your thoughts to His Word, starting with these bits of biblical descriptions that are true about you:

- ✥ A new creation (2 Cor. 5:17)

- ✥ Not condemned (Rom. 8:1)

- ✥ Holy and dearly loved (Col. 3:12)

Jesus died to give us an abundant life of freedom and hope, not shame and unbelief. Today, ask God to wash the hurt and regret from your sin away with the transforming power of His truth. And pray for a heart and mind that accept and believe the freedom of God's grace and forgiveness. Our failures are never more powerful than our God. Let Him define who you are.

> **Dear Lord,**
>
> *By faith I accept Your forgiveness and refuse to be defined*
> *any longer by my sin that You've already forgiven.*
> *Today, I confess and move on! I will define myself by Your transforming truth*
> *so that I can live fully and freely in Your grace.*
>
> *In Jesus's Name, Amen.*

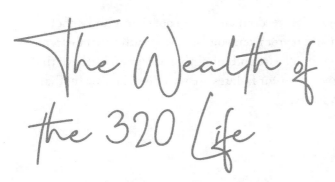

The Wealth of the 320 Life

IMMEASURABLY MORE THAN WE CAN ASK OR IMAGINE

Have you ever wondered or even asked out loud, "Is this as good as it gets?" Your dreams are still only dreams, and the expectation of what you thought your life would look like is very different from the reality you are living. Perhaps your life resembles a hamster running on the wheel in its cage: serving, giving, supervising, and organizing. Week after week, you sit in church taking notes and singing praise songs, yet you sense there is something more and you've somehow missed it. Others seem to be thriving in their relationship with Christ, despite their sufferings and misfortunes, but you can't seem to gain any momentum.

This pretty much describes my life two decades ago. I thought I must have missed the Sunday the preacher taught on how to have an intimate and thriving relationship with Jesus, but that hardly seemed possible. My salvation experience started when I was a young girl. I grew up in the church; you name it, I attended it—Sunday school, Training Union, GAs (Girls in Action), children's choir, youth choir, and youth camp. With all this training, how could I have missed the vitally important teaching about having a wonderfully exciting, peaceful, and confident faith-filled life with the Man who had died to save me?

Jesus died. He rose again. I believed it. I was saved. Isn't that all there was to it? The answer is no. The Christian life is so much more than Calvary.

> *Every believer is made for more. We're made to live a life full of grace, mercy, love, and forgiveness.*

Christ's sacrifice on Calvary was the price He paid for us to have a life that is full, abundant, and free. But for us to believe that our faith journey begins and ends at

Calvary is to cheapen the high price Christ paid. If salvation were the only part of the plan, when we accepted Christ as our Savior, we would go immediately to Heaven. This was not the plan. Every believer is made for more; we're made to live a life full of grace, mercy, love, and forgiveness . . . a life to serve others and to make Heaven crowded by living out God's love. Others should see Christ in us, and God will draw them to Himself, so they accept Christ as their Savior. If you're thinking, *"Yes! That's the life I've always wanted and wondered how to have,"* then you're looking for the 320 Life.

To introduce you to this life, we are going to dive into the Bible verse upon which my books *Yes, No and Maybe: Living with the God of Immeasurably More* and *The 320 Life: The Life You Always Wanted and Wondered How to Have* were written. That Bible verse is Ephesians 3:20. We'll look at it more below, but let's quickly meet its author and audience.

Ephesus was a capital city in the Roman province of Asia Minor. The apostle Paul spent two years of his second missionary journey there, evangelizing and teaching about Jesus. God worked through Paul's tireless efforts to bring many to faith in Christ and to establish a church there. Several years after his visit to Ephesus, Paul wrote a letter to the Ephesian church.

> *"It is impossible to petition God for too much because His capacity to give far exceeds the believer's ability to ask or imagine."*

In Ephesians chapter three, Paul encouraged the church to let their spiritual roots grow deep. The apostle sent a heartfelt prayer, in which he asked God to give the Ephesians strength through the Holy Spirit, faith in Christ, knowledge of His vast love, and for them to be "filled to the measure of all the fullness of God" (Eph. 3:19 [NIV]).

These requests may seem like a tall order and a lot to ask, but "Paul was teaching his readers what he himself already knew, that it is impossible to petition God for too much because His capacity to give far exceeds the believer's ability to ask or imagine." Maybe it was this knowledge that caused Paul to break out in joyful praise to—and an amazing declaration about—God at the end of this chapter in verse twenty!

For fun, and because we are Word-lovin' believers, I've included several translations below of Paul's worshipful words to read. (This will be the norm for each week's verse.) Scripture is so fun to study!

Ephesians 3:20

"Now all glory to God, who is able, through his mighty power at work within us, to accomplish infinitely more than we might ask or think." (NLT)

"Now to Him Who, by (in consequence of) the [action of His] power that is at work within us, is able to [carry out His purpose and] do superabundantly, far over and above all that we [dare] ask or think [infinitely beyond our highest prayers, desires, thoughts, hopes, or dreams]." (AMPC)

"Now glory be to God, who by his mighty power at work within us is able to do far more than we would ever dare to ask or even dream of—infinitely beyond our highest prayers, desires, thoughts, or hopes." (TLB)

"Now to him who is able to do far more abundantly than all that we ask or think, according to the power at work within us." (ESV)

No matter how it's worded, that is an amazing promise from God! It applied to the Ephesians back then, and it still applies to Christ followers today. Are you ready to embrace this 320 Life, which is more than you could dream of or hope for?

Side note: I just LOVE reading all translations of the Bible! Which do you like best? My favorite to study is the NLT (New Living Translation). I personally don't think God has a translation preference (when I get to Heaven, He may correct me). In my heart of hearts, I believe He is just delighted when His children study, live, and obey His Word, no matter which version they read. So, as we spend the next 4 weeks studying the 320 Life, choose any translation that you want to read, study, and memorize.

Something to Pursue

STUDYING AND LEARNING PSALM 119

Our world is full of worthless things, comparatively speaking, to what the 320 Immeasurably More Life offers. All the bells and whistles, and everything that glistens and glitters, are purposely placed by Satan—the prince of this world (John 12:31)—to distract us from the life Christ died to give us. Turning our eyes away from what *seems* pleasing, beautiful, and harmless isn't easy. The apostle Paul knew this full well.

Paul's pre-Jesus and post-Jesus lives looked radically different from one other. Pre-Jesus Paul (a.k.a. Saul) seemed to have it all. He came from a prestigious family heritage, received the best schooling and earned academic achievements, held a prominent place in his community, and had pull with the high priest. With such pedigree and power, Saul found success in whatever he put his hand to. At the time we meet him in Scripture, Saul had one thing in his sights: to persecute Christians. Little did he know that God had Saul in His sights. Saul's life was about to change forever.

As Saul and his regiment of men marched toward Damascus with their eyes on the prize of ending Christianity, Jesus stopped him in his tracks. He appeared to Saul in a light so bright that it blinded the soon-to-be-convert. Not only was Saul's physical eyesight changed from his encounter with Christ, but his spiritual eyesight was also. Saul found himself on the brink of the 320 Life. He'd soon trade the meaningless things of this world—the clout, empty ambition, and material wealth—for spiritual riches beyond his wildest dreams (he would also trade the name Saul for Paul).

Experiencing the 320 Life requires discipline, intentionality,
and a trust relationship with the Lord.

Experiencing the 320 Life requires discipline, intentionality, and a trust relationship with the Lord. As we grow in those areas, we'll be able to pray as the psalmist did when he asked God to "turn my eyes from worthless things, and give me life through your word" (Ps. 119:37 [NLT]). This is exactly what happened to Saul when Jesus met him that day. He'd been heading down a road of death and was now on the way to new life. He went from persecuting to preaching, from self-gratification to Christ glorification. As God turned Paul's focus from worthless, worldly ways, he lived out the very words that he would eventually pray for the Ephesians: "I pray that the eyes of your heart may be enlightened in order that you may know the hope to which he has called you, the riches of his glorious inheritance in his holy people, and his incomparably great power for us who believe" (Eph. 1:18–19 [NIV]).

Take note of what road you are walking; where are your eyes and heart focused? Personalize both Psalm 119:37 and Ephesians 1:18–19 for yourself and pray for the power of the Holy Spirit to help you turn your eyes from the things of this world to the wonderful ways of God. As you do, you will grow in confident faith and unshakeable devotion to God and His Word, and you'll receive the wonderful 320 Life that He has promised.

Challenge Verse: Psalm 119:37

Highlight and write down your favorite translation of this week's verse on an index card or a piece of paper. Post the card on your mirror where you get ready every day, next to your favorite chair, or by your coffee maker so you can read it frequently. This will help you learn the verse and put it into practice. Be sure to see Appendix 2 in the back of this book for more Bible verse memorization tips.

- ❖ "Turn my eyes from worthless things, and give me life through your word." (NLT)

- ❖ "Turn away mine eyes from beholding vanity, and quicken Thou me in Thy way." (KJ21)

- ❖ "Turn away my eyes from beholding vanity (idols and idolatry); and restore me to vigorous life *and* health in Your ways." (AMPC)

- ❖ "Divert my eyes from toys and trinkets, invigorate me on the pilgrim way." (THE MESSAGE)

Something to Hold Onto

IMMEASURABLY MORE STATEMENT

We all have little quips or quotes we know, even if we don't remember where we learned them. "A penny saved is a penny earned." "Many hands make light work." "Do unto others as you'd have them do unto you." "Life is like a box of chocolates." (Okay, we probably remember where we know the last two from!) These short sentences stick in our memory for multiple reasons: they help us remember a larger point, they're inspiring, and they're encouraging.

That's why I'm sharing these Something to Hold Onto sections with you. Each week, you'll be given an Immeasurably More statement to help you grab hold of the week's main topic. These memory markers will help you anchor your thoughts on the study now, and, later, they'll help you recall the truths you learned.

Feel free to write these statements out on a notecard or in your journal, along with our Something to Pursue challenge Bible verses.

The life you always wanted to live begins with yes to God.

One day it dawned on me: I rarely consulted God about His will when I prayed. And I prayed a lot. I'd send about 100 haphazard prayers up to Heaven throughout my busy day, but I never actually listened in return. I didn't ask what His will for my day (much less for my life) was. I didn't seek His guidance or wisdom. I didn't know the Word well enough to align my heart with His.

I didn't like the state of my prayer life, so I started to carve out time to spend with Jesus and to study Scripture. Instead of my rushed, one-way praying, I quieted my mind and waited on God to speak to me. And I took time to read the Bible and learn about His ways. Can I be honest? When I began to recognize the Holy Spirit's promptings and learned what Scripture instructed me to do . . . well, I didn't necessarily want to obey.

Obeying required me to change and to give up things that I loved: personal time, pride, a well-organized schedule, sin, sleep . . . and the list went on. My first reaction was *No, I don't want to do that*. But then I noticed a funny thing happen. The more time I spent with Jesus in prayer and deepened my understanding of His ways, the less I wanted to hold onto my time, pride, sleep, etc. The more time I spent with Jesus, the more I grew in confidence of hearing His voice and knowing His heart. Then, as I found myself in situations where God would prompt me to do something that I normally would have wanted to say *no* to, I had the confidence and desire to readily say *yes*. Saying *yes* to God has required me to give up a lot, but the trade-off has been worth it!

Every time we say *yes* to God, we take another step in the 320 Life. A life that is more than we could dream of, pray for, or imagine. Let's take a minute to let that soak in . . . then praise God for His goodness. Say it along with Paul: "Now all glory to God, who is able, through his mighty power at work within us, to accomplish infinitely more than we might ask or think" (Eph. 3:20 [NLT]). The life we always wanted to live begins with yes to God—a life where God answers our prayers and grants our desires, because they're aligned with His.

Something to View

VIDEO LISTENING GUIDE

My favorite fast-food restaurant is Chick-fil-A, and my favorite entrée is an 8-pack chicken nugget with two packs of BBQ sauce for dipping. *Mm-mmm!* Are you drooling? As soon as I sit down, I open my pack to count the miniature chicken delights. Most of the time, I count eight; however, every now and then, the red-shirted food preparer packs nine (and on the rare occasion 10) nuggets. When I get a bonus nugget, warmth swells inside me from my head to my toes. It really is the little things in life that thrill a soul, isn't it?

So, what's the big deal about an extra nugget or two? I'm glad you asked. The life that Christ died to give you can be likened to the extra nuggets in the pack.

Pause.

Hang with me. I promise I'm going somewhere. It is not my intention to cheapen the cost of the cross by comparing Jesus's ultimate sacrifice to a box of nuggets. This is simply to give you a rudimentary example to which you can relate. I am confident you will be able to relate, even if you don't like chicken nuggets.

Unpause.

When I place an order for an 8-count chicken nugget entrée, and I am given two extra ones, I'm thrilled. Did I pay for these freebies? Did I do anything to deserve them? The correct answer is no. Somehow that makes those two bonus nuggets taste even better than the other eight. I feel so happy and can't wait to tell some-one about my extras.

The 320 Life is filled with extras. There are too many to count, and most remain a mystery until you happen upon them. You don't pay for the extras, nor have you done anything to deserve them. How do we receive these added bonuses? Paul gives us the answer: "But God is so rich in mercy; he loved us so much that even though we were spiritually dead and doomed by our sins, he gave us back our lives again when he raised Christ from the dead—only by his undeserved favor have we ever been saved—and lifted us up from the grave into glory along with Christ, where we sit with him in the heavenly realms—all because of what Christ Jesus did" (Eph. 2:4–6 [TLB]).

We were made to live more with this God. This God is the God of Immeasurably More. Not more stuff, more money, more followers on social media, more houses, more cars . . . not more as the world defines more. We were made to be the dwelling place of God through the person of the Holy Spirit and to produce and enjoy more of His loving traits: love, joy, peace, patience, goodness, kindness, gentleness, faithfulness, and self-control (see Galatians 5:22–23). We were made for the 320 Life! Maybe the chicken nugget example isn't registering with you, so let's chat more about it. First, let's look at what the 320 Life *is not* and what it *is*.

What the 320 Life is *not*?

- ❖ A bunch of rules.

- ❖ Getting all the _____ things _____.

- ❖ Working for salvation.

- ❖ The more I do, the more I'm blessed _____.

What *is* the 320 Life?

- ❖ It's living _____ with complete _____ and _____ that everything that happens is sovereignly planned, because you love God, not because you want more and more from Him.

- ❖ Greater than the sum of your:
  past _____ and experiences.
  hopes and _____.
  bank _____.
  titles and _____.

Immeasurably more comes from a compound Greek word meaning:

- ❖ For the sake of, more, and beyond

- ❖ Exceeding some number, measure, rank, or need

- ❖ Over and above, more than is necessary (this is my favorite part of the definition)

Some Bible translators express the phrase as "superabundantly more." God is able to do superabundantly more than we can ask or imagine.

The 320 Life is complete surrender

- ❖ to a God you can't _____ .

- ❖ to experience the _____ and
  _____ .

"God can do anything, you know—far more than you could ever imagine or guess or request in your wildest dreams! He does it not by pushing us around but by working within us, his Spirit deeply and gently within us." Eph. 3:20 (THE MESSAGE)

We have the same all access pass to peace, power, joy, and grace.

I love the encouragement that Bible scholar Warren Wiersbe gives in his commentary on Ephesians 3:20: "Get your hands on your spiritual wealth by opening your heart to the Holy Spirit, and praying with Paul for strength for the inner man . . . for a new depth of love . . . for spiritual apprehension . . . and for spiritual fullness." I'll paraphrase Mr. Wiersbe's awesome quote below—it is upon this that we are going to build our case for the 320 Life:

> *We get our hands on our spiritual wealth by opening our hearts to God.*

Our spiritual wealth is found when we say:

- ❖ *yes* to God, because yes cultivates trust _____ God.

- ❖ *no* to self, because no invites revelation _____ God.

- ❖ *maybe* to others, because *maybe* welcomes freedom _____ God.

Oh, the treasures we find when we live by God's ways! His wealth doesn't compare to anything this world can offer. Let Psalm 119:37 be your prayer: "Turn my eyes from worthless things, and give me life through your Word" (NLT).

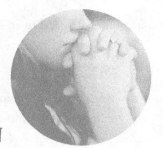

Devotion

CAMPING TOO CLOSE TO SIN

"Abram settled in the land of Canaan, while Lot settled among the cities of the valley and moved his tent as far as Sodom."

Gen. 13:12 (ESV)

Growing up in the 1970s, I had plenty of new styles of dance clubs, alcohol, and drugs to be tempted by. Thankfully, my parents faithfully guided me away from those. In particular, I remember one saying they repeated as a warning of potential dangers of hanging out with the wrong crowd or going places I shouldn't: "If you play with fire, you are going to get burned."

Throughout Scripture, we see many people play with fire and reap the painful consequences: Eve with the forbidden fruit, King David with Bathsheba, the Israelites with foreign idols. But an example that interests me is Lot with his land.

Genesis tells us the story of Lot and Abraham, Lot's uncle. They, along with their families, herds, and servants, all lived together until both camps grew so large, they needed their own space. Abraham suggested that they part ways amicably, and he offered Lot first choice of where to set up his new home. "So Lot chose for himself all the Jordan Valley, and Lot journeyed east. Thus, they separated from each other. Abram settled in the land of Canaan, while Lot settled among the cities of the valley and moved his tent as far as Sodom" (Gen. 13:11–12 [ESV]).

Did you notice where Lot moved? Sodom. Yes, the infamous Sodom from Sodom and Gomorrah. A place rank with sin, debauchery, and wickedness. Now, when he chose that area, I don't believe Lot intended to be so close to or fall into the immorality in Sodom. I think Lot picked that lush and beautiful valley because it was a wonderful place to raise livestock.

However, Sodom and Gomorrah were infiltrated and consumed with evil. Eventually these cities found themselves at war with several enemies, one of which captured and imprisoned Lot and his family. Upon hearing this news, Abraham heroically led over 300 men of his own household against Lot's kidnappers. He pursued and defeated Lot's enemy, rescuing Lot, his family and household, and his possessions.

Despite his uncle's extreme efforts and valiant rescue, despite knowing the dangers and wickedness of Sodom, despite almost losing his life and all that he loved and owned—*Lot moved back to Sodom!*

Lot's choice may seem foolish and baffling to some, but I understand his decision to return to the "edge of sin." If I do not keep my guard up, I can easily find myself heading back to the same sin camp over and over. Why? Temptation is strong. Sin feels good; if it didn't, we would not keep going near it. This is how the enemy traps us. But we have to keep in mind that playing with sin will always hurt us. *If we play with fire, we are going to get burned.*

God loves us so much; He doesn't want us anywhere close to sin or to bear its consequences. He will bring destruction—sooner or later—to the means of the sin in our lives. He did this for Lot. Because the sin of the people in Sodom and Gomorrah was so grievous, God set out to destroy them; but out of His love for Abraham (and I believe His love for Lot too), He sent angels to rescue Lot and his family first. Once they were out of the city, God rained down destruction on Sodom and Gomorrah (Genesis 19), and Lot had to find a new place to live. What can we take away from Lot camping too close to sin?

> **We are bound to be seduced by sin.** Sometimes we like to live right on the edge of sin and flirt with it. The enemy entices us while we're on the edge, hoping we will cross over and stay a while. "Be sober-minded; be watchful. Your adversary the devil prowls around like a roaring lion, seeking someone to devour. Resist him, firm in your faith . . . " 1 Pet. 5:8–9 (ESV)

> **God will give us an opportunity to be rescued from temptation.** "The temptations in your life are no different from what others experience. And God is faithful. He will not allow the temptation to be more than you can stand. When you are tempted, he will show you a way out so that you can endure."
> 1 Cor. 10:13 (NLT)

> **It is hard to reach out and accept the rescue.** The grip of the stronghold of sin becomes tighter and tighter with each passing day of living on the edge. "But each person is tempted when he is lured and enticed by his own desire.

Then desire when it has conceived gives birth to sin, and sin when it is fully grown brings forth death." James 1:14–15 (ESV)

Once we are rescued, we don't look back. The first time Lot was rescued, he went back to the "edge of sin." In the second rescue, his wife looked back and turned into a pillar of salt. Once we are rescued, we don't look back; instead, we need to look toward our freedom. "Everyone who makes a practice of sinning also practices lawlessness; sin is lawlessness. You know that he appeared in order to take away sins, and in him there is no sin. No one who abides in him keeps on sinning . . . " 1 John 3:4–6 (ESV)

What about you? Have you chosen to pitch your tent in an area that is lush and green, but also too close to sin? Perhaps it is at the water cooler where workday conversations are inappropriate. Or maybe you are looking in the wrong place for "Mr. Right." Has the mommy-and-me playgroup become too gossipy? Are you too close to the edge of sin? Ask God to rescue you, and when you leave, don't look back.

Dear Lord,

Forgive me for staying too close to the edge of sin.
I need Your help to leave my current camp. Will You come and rescue me?
Thank You for always being there when I need You.

In Jesus's Name, Amen.

Something to Do

STUDY QUESTIONS

1. Have you ever experienced an "Is this as good as it gets?" moment? What were the circumstances surrounding this moment?

_____

_____

_____

2. Which translation of Ephesians 3:20 is your favorite? Write it in the space below.

_____

_____

_____

3. In the space below, write the *Yes, No, and Maybe* statements.

_____

_____

_____

4. Turn to Ephesians 3 in your Bible. In verses 16–19, Paul tells the church he prays for them. What does he pray?

_____

_____

_____

5. What excites you the most about this *320 Life* study?

6. What obstacles have kept you from pursuing the Lord wholeheartedly?

7. How desperate are you to open your heart so you can *get your hands on the spiritual wealth* of God? What sacrifices are you willing to make?

8. Take a moment to write a prayer. I've helped you start it with a few words from one of my favorite people in the Bible, King David. He wrote the following in Psalm 139:23–24:

    "Search me, O God, and know my heart; test me and know my anxious thoughts. Point out anything in me that offends you, and lead me along the path of everlasting life." (NLT)

    Personalize the words of Paul's prayer in Ephesians 3:16–19, then end your prayer with your own paraphrase of verse twenty.

JOURNAL ENTRY BETWEEN YOU AND JESUS

Use this space to journal what you hear from the Lord in your time of prayer and what you learn as you study God's Word. It may be that you offer God adoration, praise, thanks, or repentance. Or it may be that God offers you encouragement, direction, correction, or healing. Don't worry about punctuation, grammar, or spelling; just write. It's all between you and Jesus.

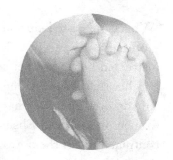

Devotion

FAITH-FULL

"What can I do to help you?' Elisha asked. 'Tell me, what do you have in the house?' 'Nothing at all, except a flask of olive oil,' she replied." 2 Kings 4:2 (NLT)

One never-ending year. Twelve difficult months. 365 faith-testing days. That's how long it had been since my husband began having serious health problems. We went to his general physician, followed all his instructions, but nothing changed. We were then referred to a specialist, whose directions we followed. Nothing changed. So, we tried a new specialist who prescribed a different medication, and still nothing changed.

Over the next few months, we were unwilling passengers on the roller coaster of uncertainty, hoping each new doctor and medication would relieve Scott's symptoms and pain. All efforts proved fruitless. The process wore us down physically, mentally, and spiritually. My faith wavered. I believed God for a miracle, but I doubted one would ever come, especially when I thought about how long we'd been praying and how many people were interceding on our behalf.

People literally around the world were praying for us. Why wasn't God, the Great Physician, answering their prayers? We only needed one miracle—why couldn't my husband have just one? In a last-ditch effort for answers—*for a miracle*—my husband prayerfully went to a specialist in another city. I was disappointed I was unable to make the trip with him, but little did I know that God had a miracle waiting for me at home.

That week, I read in 2 Kings 4 of a desperate woman who was long on sorrows and short on faith. I saw myself in between the lines of this widow's story. In his lifetime, the woman's husband had accrued a sizeable debt that the widow could not pay after his death. To satisfy that debt, the authorities threatened to take her sons as slaves. With what little faith she had, the widow shared her sorrows with the prophet Elisha. She believed he was the one person who could help her; she was right.

"'What can I do to help you?' Elisha asked. 'Tell me, what do you have in the house?' 'Nothing at all, except a flask of olive oil,' she replied" (2 Kings 4:2 [NLT]). Elisha instructed her to ask her sons to borrow empty jars from her neighbors. He then told her that from the one flask of olive oil she had left, God would miraculously fill the other jars, so that she could sell the oil to pay her husband's debt. The women obeyed, and Elisha's words proved true. Miraculously, her one flask of oil continued to fill the borrowed jars until there were no more empty jars left. After the widow and her sons had filled the jars, she went back to Elisha to ask for further instructions. He told her, "Now sell the olive oil and pay your debts, and you and your sons can live on what is left over" (vv. 7 [NLT]).

As I pondered on this widow's desperate plight, God instructed me to follow her example. He asked me to bring my figurative "empty jars" of faith to the altar at the close of the church service the following Sunday morning. I did not understand, nor did I want to obey. I was long on sorrows and short on faith.

Throughout the week, I felt God's nearness and His prompting to bring my empty jars to Him. Throughout the week, I continued to tell Him no. I was afraid others would make a fuss over me at the altar, but that God wouldn't notice me at all. I did not want to be disappointed again.

Sunday morning came, and I was still arguing with the Lord as I sat down in the pew. Imagine my surprise as the pastor said, "Open your Bibles to 2 Kings 4." God had indeed arranged a miracle for me. The miracle wasn't to heal my husband, but to heal my faith; He had arranged to fill my emptiness with a new faith that I would carry throughout the journey of my husband's uncertain future.

At the close of the sermon, with fear and trembling, I took my "empty jars" to the altar. The moment was personal with the Lord and precious. Although the church was full, it felt as if only the Lord and I were in the sanctuary. I walked into church that morning faith-less and walked out faith-*full*.

Do you desire to be faith-full? If you are long on sorrows and short on faith, gather your empty jars and take them to the only One who can help you. The Lord will meet you there. It will be personal and precious. He will fill you with enough faith to get you through the known and the unknown. Only God can make you faith-full.

Dear Lord,

I believe in You, help me to believe You.

I bring You my empty jars of faith, asking You to make me faith-full.

I don't want to be a woman long on sorrows and short on faith anymore.

I know You are the only One who can help me.

In Jesus's Name, Amen.

Week 2

THE WEALTH
OF *YES*

The Immeasurably More Life
is found at the intersection of
God's Word and our obedience to it.

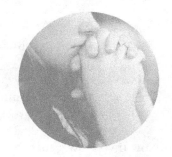

Devotion

JESUS CHAIR

"The Sovereign Lord has given me a well-instructed tongue, to know the word that sustains the weary. He wakens me morning by morning, wakens my ear to listen like one being instructed."

Isa. 50:4 (NIV)

If I were to show you a snapshot of myself 20 years ago, you'd see an unhappy person, struggling in her faith and failing to be the godly woman she knew God had asked her to be. She spoke rudely to her family. She judged others unfairly. And she responded harshly when life didn't go her way.

Around this time, I heard Isaiah 50:4, "The Sovereign Lord has given me a well-instructed tongue, to know the word that sustains the weary. He wakens me morning by morning, wakens my ear to listen like one being instructed" (NIV). When I read the word weary, it resonated in my heart. I remember thinking, *I'm weary. I need sustaining.*

As I re-read this verse, I longed for the sustaining part—it sounded comforting; however, I did not care for the morning wake-up call. I didn't want to wake up earlier than I already had to, but I knew it was the only way I could spend time with God in my full schedule. I figured, *I can't get much wearier than I already am, so why not?*

The next morning, the sun rose and so did I, grumbling . . . a lot! I could hardly see through my sleepy eyes, but day after day, I would drag myself out of bed, curl up in the same place I call my "Jesus chair," and I'd pray and read my Bible. My early morning meetings with God felt rehearsed and ridged, nothing like what I expected when my weary heart was first gripped by that verse in Isaiah.

Even though I felt discouraged, I was determined to continue. Every morning, I'd shuffle to my Jesus chair with my Bible and devotion book. And then, almost without noticing, my heart started to soften. I looked forward to my time in God's

Word and prayer. As I shifted my focus from myself to the presence of God, my weariness started to subside. God's Word took root in my heart, and I was experiencing its sustaining power.

There was less complaining and more contentment. My ears began to listen like one being instructed, just like the verse in Isaiah says.

Now if you saw a snapshot of me, you'd see a cheerful wife and mom, greeting her family with a smile in the morning. You'd find a friend who doesn't jump to conclusions about others. You'd catch a woman speaking words of praise in moments of panic.

If you were to share a snapshot of yourself with me, what would I see? A woman looking for a word to sustain her weary soul? Someone desperate enough to dedicate time each day in God's Word and in prayer? For me, it must be in the morning in my Jesus chair, before the rush of life's demands. For you, it may be in the front seat of your car with your Bible during your daughter's ballet class. Maybe your Jesus chair is at your desk with a devotional book. Or it may be on a park bench as you eat lunch and pray.

Wherever and whenever you meet with God doesn't really matter; it only matters that you spend time together each day. His Word is our sustaining power. Pick your Jesus chair, get your Bible (and maybe a devotional book), and listen like one being taught. God has much to say.

Dear Lord,

Thank You for Your Word that sustains my weary soul.
I commit to set aside time to read Scripture each day.
Help me to quiet my mind and to listen like one being taught.

In Jesus's Name, Amen.

The Wealth of Yes

YES CULTIVATES TRUST IN GOD

In week 1, we read an amazing quote by renowned Bible theologian Warren Wiersbe. Let's refresh ourselves with our paraphrase of what Mr. Wiersbe said of Paul's phrase in Ephesians 3:20 of "immeasurably more than all we ask or imagine" (NIV): *We get our hands on our spiritual wealth by opening our hearts to God.*

Spiritual wealth can't be compared to material wealth and all that the world offers us. In fact, it can scarcely be put into words. It's not found in a check list of dos and don'ts. Spiritual wealth is accumulated by our intimate experiences with our Savior and God, through the power of the indwelling Holy Spirit. This kind of wealth is amassed by walking rightly in the fullness of His presence, being directed by the authority of His Word—committed to saying *yes* to all its principles—and completely submitting to the Holy Spirit.

The wealth He gives has no end. There is an abundance of all we need. Personal wants and wishes are no longer a concern for those who have opened their hearts to God and gotten their hands on the spiritual wealth of immeasurably more. There is an explicit and inexplicable trust in the truth of Philippians 4:19, "And this same God who takes care of me will supply all your needs from his glorious riches, which have been given to us in Christ Jesus" (NLT), which fuels the trust of every *yes* we utter to God.

> *Our spiritual wealth is found when we open our heart*
> *and say yes to God, because . . .*
> *Yes cultivates trust in God.*

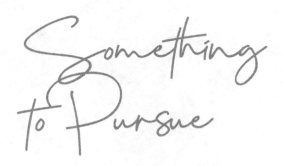

STUDYING AND LEARNING PSALM 119

Let's open our Bibles to Psalm 119:60, where you can almost feel the excitement of the psalmist as he writes: "I will hurry, without delay, to obey your commands" (NLT). The apostle Paul's life exemplified this verse. After his encounter with Jesus on the road to Damascus, Paul hurried, without delay, to obey Jesus's commands. He didn't debate himself or others over if he had really seen Jesus; he didn't dilly-dally over being baptized; and he didn't argue with others over if it was safe to preach Christ crucified and risen. No, Paul simply responded yes to God, without delay. "Saul spent a few days getting acquainted with the Damascus disciples, but then *went right to work, wasting no time,* preaching in the meeting places that this Jesus was the Son of God" (Acts 9:19–20 [THE MESSAGE], emphasis added).

> *Our confidence in obedience-without-delay grows as*
> *we grow in our knowledge of Scripture.*

How do you respond to God? Is your knee-jerk reply to His instruction usually, *But, God, I'm busy, tired, sad, not smart enough, scared . . .?* Or, *I'll begin that Bible study next week. Do You really want me to check on the widow next door? I'll start to pray with my children when they're older.* Our hesitation in obeying God or questioning His commands is an indication that we trust ourselves more than Him. Our confidence in obedience-without-delay grows as we grow in our knowledge of Scripture. As we align our actions with God's Word, we build trust in the Lord.

If you find yourself being slow to obey God—when you know what He's asking you to do, and it aligns with His Word—confess that to Him and ask for His help to hurry to say yes. Then you'll be able to do as the psalmist and Paul did. You'll obey without delay.

Challenge Verse: Psalm 119:60

Highlight and write down your favorite translation of this week's verse on an index card or a piece of paper. Post the card on your mirror where you get ready every day, next to your favorite chair, or by your coffee maker so you can read it frequently. This will help you learn the verse and put it into practice.

- ❖ "I will hurry, without delay, to obey your commands." (NLT)

- ❖ "I made haste and delayed not to keep Your commandments." (AMPC)

- ❖ "As soon as you command, I do what you say." (CEV)

- ❖ "I was up at once, didn't drag my feet, was quick to follow your orders." (THE MESSAGE)

Something to Hold Onto

IMMEASURABLY MORE STATEMENT

The Immeasurably More Life is found at the intersection of God's Word and our obedience to it.

Years ago, the Lord whispered to my heart to stop watching a certain television show. I would love to say that I immediately obeyed Him with a glad heart, fully confident that He had my best interest in mind, but I can't.

I couldn't see a possible reason why I shouldn't tune in. My watching this show wasn't causing anyone to stumble in their walk with the Lord. I was not influencing others to watch it; in fact, my family was all in bed. The show itself wasn't glorifying sin. And watching it didn't keep me from getting my work and chores done. It was my time. Time set aside each week for just me. What possible reason could the Lord have for asking me to stop?

Under the conviction of the Holy Spirit, I realized the audacity of my attitude and understood my egotistical reasoning. I thought since I had been obeying God in other areas of life that I had the "right" to negotiate His other instructions. I finally saw the fallacy of my justifications. You see, the Immeasurably More Life is found at the intersection of God's Word and our obedience to it. I knew that Deuteronomy 5:33 told me to "walk in obedience to *all* that the LORD your God has commanded you" (NIV, emphasis added), not just what I felt made sense. Even though I was obeying in other things, I was willfully disobeying Him by continuing to watch that show.

In doing so, *I* was the person I was causing to stumble. It's not that watching television or enjoying that show were sins, but my staying up late was making me sleep in the next morning. I would then miss my time of prayer and reading Scripture. This would snowball into rushing to get ready, snapping at my kids, and being too tired to listen to God throughout the day. By not turning off the television at night, I wasn't tuning into Him the next morning.

Is God asking you to give up something, so that you can spend more time with Him in prayer and reading Scripture? If we're going to be ready each morning to wake up and obey His Word, we need to prepare the night before. We can't begin to imagine what God wants to do in, through, and for us as we obey all He has commanded us.

VIDEO LISTENING GUIDE

The Immeasurably More Life is found at the intersection of God's Word and our obedience to it. The wealth of yes cannot be found apart from submission to God and obedience to His Word. You will discover that His truth is countercultural and even counter-Church. Sadly, there are divisions within the large Church, denominations, and regional/local churches about the validity and application of God's Word.

Though this news is shocking, many in the Bible prophesied regarding the subject. Jude, the brother of Jesus, warned: "But you, my dear friends, must remember what the apostles of our Lord Jesus Christ predicted. They told you that in the last times there would be scoffers whose purpose in life is to satisfy their ungodly desires. These people are the ones who are creating divisions among you. They follow their natural instincts because they do not have God's Spirit in them" (Jude 17–19 [NLT]).

He also wrote this encouragement: "But you, dear friends, must build each other up in your most holy faith, pray in the power of the Holy Spirit, and await the mercy of our Lord Jesus Christ, who will bring you eternal life. In this way, you will keep yourselves safe in God's love" (Jude 20–21 [NLT]).

The life you've always wanted and wondered how to have is found at the _____ of God's Word and your _____ to it.

The life you always wanted starts with a _____.

A God-willed life starts with *yes*; *yes* means love and is clearly defined in John 14:15, "If you love me, obey my commandments" (NLT).

Love God with a _____.

But what if I don't read well and have a hard time understanding the Bible?

Ask God for _____.

Turn to Psalm 119:34

"Give me _____ and I will obey your instructions; I will put them into practice with all my heart." (NLT)

But what if I'm slow to learn?

Turn to Psalm 119:73

"You made me; you created me. Now give me the _____ to follow your commands." (NLT)

Every *yes!*

❖ *Yes* brings joy.

"Joyful are people of integrity, who follow the instructions of the Lord. Joyful are those who obey his laws and search for him with all their hearts." Ps. 119:1–2 (NLT)

❖ *Yes* gives _____.

"I will walk in freedom, for I have devoted myself to your commandments."

Ps. 119:45 (NLT)

❖ *Yes* gives life.

"I will never forget your commandments, for by them you give me life."

Ps. 119:93 (NLT)

❖ *Yes* gives strength.

"Therefore, be careful to obey every command I am giving you today, so you may have strength to go in and take over the land you are about to enter." Deut. 11:8 (NLT)

What if God asks something that is hard for me?

"For this is the love of God, that we keep His commandments; and His command-ments are not _____." 1 John 5:3 (NASB)

I'm confused about what to do.

Always err on the side of _____.

God will never ask you to do anything that is opposition to His Word, His ways, or His character.

> *"The answer to spiritual confusion is obedience."*
> —Oswald Chambers

Obey. Obey. Obey.

"God can do anything, you know—far more than you could ever imagine or guess or request in your wildest dreams! He does it not by pushing us around but by working within us, his Spirit deeply and gently within us." Eph. 3:20 (THE MESSAGE)

Devotion

DARE TO HOPE

"Yet I still dare to hope when I remember this." Lam. 3:21 (NLT)

One word summed up a hard season in my life: hopeless. I won't ever forget those long nights of crying myself to sleep, believing that everything I'd hoped for was lost and my situation was hopeless. As I lay curled in a ball under my covers, some nights my tears fell silently; other nights I sobbed loudly. Every night I had the same questions and prayers. *"Why, Lord? What am I doing wrong? Why won't You fix this?"* I ended every prayer with, *"If it is Your will,"* in the hopes that God's will was different than what my circumstances were indicating.

At some point in all our lives, it's likely that we will find ourselves in a hopeless situation. The reasonings and magnitudes will vary, but the feelings of hopelessness will be similar. Jeremiah, known as the weeping prophet, found himself in a hopeless situation.

God used Jeremiah to prophesy to the people of Judah and Jerusalem. The Lord chose Jeremiah to tell His people of their immediate future—and it was dismal. The only things on their horizon were their discipline and the destruction of Jerusalem and God's holy Temple. God gave Jeremiah bold words to speak to His people. Jeremiah obeyed and gave the people God's truth; in turn, the people gave Jeremiah punishment, ridicule, insults, and imprisonment.

Not only was the Israelite's future grim, so was Jeremiah's. He grieved for Jerusalem and for God's people, his countrymen. In anguish, the weeping prophet lamented the words, "Everything I had hoped for from the LORD is lost" (Lam. 3:18 [NLT]).

As he sat heartbroken and hopeless, Jeremiah cried until no more tears would come (Lam. 2:11). Then, out of the midst of his despair, he shifted his focus onto the Lord. He remembered something that helped him dare to hope in the face of a hopeless situation.

Like I said, at some point in all our lives, we will each feel hopeless. But we don't have to stay stuck there. Would you like the courage to dare to hope again, regardless of your circumstances? Would you like your perspective changed on your present situation? If yes, then it would serve you well to know what Jeremiah remembered.

Read Lamentations 3:21–24 and see if you notice how the expression in Jeremiah's tone changes from grief to optimism. Can you picture his facial features transforming? "Yet I still dare to hope when I remember this: The faithful love of the LORD never ends! His mercies never cease. Great is his faithfulness; his mercies begin afresh each morning. I say to myself, 'The LORD is my inheritance; therefore, I will hope in him'" (NLT)!

What Jeremiah remembered was the key to elevating him from the pit of despair to a place of expectancy. It is our key as well. Jeremiah remembered these facts about the Lord, a covenant keeper:

- His unfailing love
- His daily new mercies
- His never-ending faithfulness
- His inheritance given to His children

God never changes. These facts that Jeremiah recalled about the Lord were true then and remain true today. Resting assured of this will transform us from the inside out. And while remembering these truths won't necessarily change our circumstances, it will change the expression in our voice and our outlook on the future. Hope means to wait with expectation, and this is what I chose to do during those hard nights in my pit of despair.

If you need hope today, re-read the facts about God that are listed above. Then be determined to remember God's love, mercy, and faithfulness . . . despite the despair and destruction around you. Will you dare to hope?

Dear Lord,

I want to dare to hope, but life seems uncertain and tentative.
Will You help me remember Your love, mercy, and faithfulness?
Thank You in advance for what You are going to do.

In Jesus's Name, Amen.

Something to Do

STUDY QUESTIONS

1. Our biggest and best *yes* to God is when we accepted His gift of salvation. Spend time walking down memory lane and write about the time you said *yes* to God and accepted His gift of salvation.

2. In this week's teaching, I make a case for obedience. Which benefit gives you the most incentive to obey God? Why?

3. Recall and write about a time you obeyed God. How did obeying God resonate with you?

4. Recall and write about a time you didn't obey God. How did disobedience make you feel? What did you do to make things right with God?

5. Based on the following definitions, would you describe your life as devoted or disloyal? (Be honest.) Give evidence to support your answer.

   Obedience can be defined as a God-willed life—a devoted life. Disobedience can be defined as a self-willed life—a disloyal life.

6. *Yes* cultivates trust in God. Holocaust survivor Corrie ten Boom once said, "Never be afraid to trust an unknown future to a known God." In what ways are you currently trusting God?

7. Sometimes we are our own biggest obstacle to growing in Christ and living a life of obedience. How do each of the "I" obstacles listed below prevent you from obeying God? How will the Bible verses enable you to hurdle any obstacles you struggle with?

Obstacle #1: I don't want to.

"For God is working in you, giving you the desire and the power to do what pleases him." Phil. 2:13 (NLT)

Obstacle #2: I am not strong enough.

"Last of all I want to remind you that your strength must come from the Lord's mighty power within you." Eph. 6:10 (TLB)

Obstacle #3: I am not good enough.

"But God shows his love for us in that while we were still sinners, Christ died for us." Rom. 5:8 (ESV)

8. On a scale of 1 to 10, how important is obedience in your relationship with God? What measures do you plan to take to increase its importance?

9. Use 1 Samuel 15:22 to answer the following question and fill in the blanks. How does God feel about obedience?

"Listen! _____ is better than sacrifice, and _____ is better than offering the fat of rams." (NLT)

10. According to Oswald Chambers, our obedience matters to other people. Ask yourself: *Am I making a positive impact on others?*

"My personal life may be crowded with small, petty happenings, altogether insignificant. But if I obey Jesus Christ in the seemingly random circumstances of life, they become pinholes through which I see the face of God. Then, when I stand face to face with God, I will discover that through my obedience thousands were blessed. When God's redemption brings a human soul to the point of obedience, it always produces. If I obey Jesus Christ, the redemption of God will flow through me to the lives of others, because behind the deed of obedience is the reality of an Almighty God."

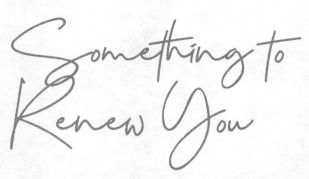

JOURNAL ENTRY BETWEEN YOU AND JESUS

Use this space to journal what you hear from the Lord in your time of prayer and what you learn as you study God's Word. It may be that you offer God adoration, praise, thanks, or repentance. Or it may be that God offers you encouragement, direction, correction, or healing. Don't worry about punctuation, grammar, or spelling; just write. It's all between you and Jesus.

Devotion

THIRTEEN WORDS THAT CHANGED MY LIFE

"Now to him who is able to do immeasurably more than all we ask or imagine, according to his power that is at work within us . . ." Eph. 3:20 (NIV)

As I cooked dinner alone, like I did most nights, the words I'd rehearsed all day played like a symphony in my head. *It was time to have a talk with my husband.* As I cleaned, I went over all the possible comebacks he could reply with—and I came up with my own retorts. As I bathed our kids and put them to bed—by myself, again—one thing ran through my mind. *Tonight is the night I talk to Scott.*

When I heard him come home and walk through the door, I hurried downstairs. We exchanged our usual "How was your day?" banter before he hurried upstairs to the den. Something had to change. The silence and distance between us had lingered for far too long. His work schedule and overtime hours were taking a toll not only on us, but on our kids too. Our children and I needed him home more, and I decided it was time to let him know that *he* needed to make some changes. Tonight was the night. I was poised and prepared for every defensive comeback he could lob my way—every comeback except for one.

With my heart pounding and my thoughts racing, I entered the room and sat beside Scott, waiting for just the right time to share my feelings. After a few minutes of forced conversation, I lunged into my lengthy, well-prepared diatribe, ending with what I thought was a showstopper: "You don't act like you ever want to come home."

All my rehearsing couldn't have prepared me to hear Scott's comeback. After a brief pause, he turned to look at me, and much to my surprise, spewed out the real showstopper: "You don't make our house a place I want to come home to."

Hanging in the air were 13 words that changed the course of my life forever. At first, I wanted to dismiss his accusation, but the thought of his words being remotely true jolted me to my core. *Did I really make our home tense, miserable, and unwelcoming?* What he'd said messed with me in the worst—and best—way. After mulling over his words for several days, I had to admit there was truth in his sentiment. I was unhappy; therefore, my life, my home, and my family were unhappy too.

Every unmet expectation, unfulfilled dream, unanswered prayer, and unwanted situation loomed larger and louder than my blessings. The *"I thought God would,"* *"I longed for God to,"* *"If only God had,"* and *"Why didn't God do?"* thoughts ran on auto-play—feeding my soul with anger, frustration, and sadness. Without realizing it, I had been operating in a negative frame of mind, hurtling from one task to the next, all the while leaving behind an unpleasant atmosphere for those around me.

Recognizing this was difficult and uneasy, yet it drove me to change the trajectory of my life. I turned to God's Word for new truths, new scripts, and a new way to approach life. His Word did not disappoint.

This new way of life started with my yes to God, which cultivated an unbreakable trust relationship with Him. Then a no to self that revealed the person I was created to be before sin and shame entered my life, as well as truth to help me transform into His image. And last, a maybe that welcomed freedom to spend my life serving God's kingdom without being overwhelmed and overcommitted.

I replaced my old scripts with new truths that will help everyone who believes them to experience life anew with the God of Immeasurably More. "Now to him who is able to do immeasurably more than all we ask or imagine, according to his power that is at work within us . . . " (Eph. 3:20 [NIV]). This is the life every believer was born to live.

Ask yourself: *Do I make my house a place my family doesn't want to come home to? What scripts run through my head? Do I leave an unpleasant atmosphere behind me?* If you answered *yes* to any of these—while I know these are not enjoyable realities to own—there is a way to turn them around.

Let go of your expectations and embrace God's will, relinquish your dreams to God's plans, pray for His ways, and accept His peace in every situation. Then, you will be able to say to your *un*met expectations: *"God will superabundantly exceed my expectations."* To your *un*fulfilled dreams, say: *"God will superabundantly surpass my dreams."* Then to your *un*answered prayers, say: *"God's answer will be superabundantly greater than I can ask."* And to your *un*wanted situations, say: *"God's resolution will be superabundantly better than mine."* Let them be the beginning of your *yes, no,* and *maybe* adventure with the God of Immeasurably More.

Oh, and about those 13 words? My husband has since replaced them with 13 new words: "You make our house a place that I *love* to come home to."

> ### Dear Lord,
>
> *I'm tired of going through the motions of the Christian life.*
>
> *I want a burning desire to know and experience You,*
> *the God of Immeasurably More.*
>
> *Please correct me when I fall back into thinking old, negative scripts.*
>
> *I want to focus on You so that I might live the life*
> *You intended for me to live.*
>
> *In Jesus's Name, Amen.*

Week 3

THE WEALTH
OF *NO*

The Immeasurably More Life
doesn't come without cost.

Devotion

ADDICTED TO SELF

> *"You must each decide in your heart how much to give.*
> *And don't give reluctantly or in response to pressure.*
> *'For God loves a person who gives cheerfully.'"* 2 Cor. 9:7 (NLT)

I love the satisfaction of completing a task. In particular, I love finishing a task that also pays me to do it. When my kids were young, I'd clean out their closets of the clothes they'd outgrown to sell the outfits at a local consignment sale. One summer stands out to me. Although I was tired from lugging bags and bags down the stairs to the front door, I was very excited to earn enough money to buy my children's clothes for the next year. *What a great feeling!* I thought. But as I stared at the bags lining my hallway, a different thought came to mind.

I felt the familiar nudge of the Holy Spirit, asking me to obey Him in something I really didn't want to do. "Give your children's clothes to Stacey." Surely, I was making that up or I hadn't heard right. After all, I aimed to be a good steward of our finances and selling at the consignment sale helped us out a lot each year. Once again, I heard the command, "Give the clothes to Stacey." *But Lord*, I argued, *I have my own children to clothe. I sell these to afford to buy new clothes for them. And I give in other ways. When someone is sick, I bring them a meal. Every Christmas, I buy gifts for the Angel Tree at church. We sponsor a young girl in Ecuador, providing food and clothes. Isn't that generous enough? After all, I must take care of my family and my needs.*

But I heard that voice again, "Give them to Stacey."

My greediness and disobedience eventually went beyond arguing. I obstinately ignored God's instructions by ignoring the bags for several days as they sat at the end of the hall. I thought by doing this, I would feel better about disobeying, but the command to give the clothes away would not go away. As it became stronger, my sinful will to disobey became weaker. After a week, I called Stacey, and we arranged a time for me to drop the clothes off at her home.

This experience was one in a long line of lessons that revealed to me a sickness I was not aware I was plagued with: I am a self-a-holic. I was way too concerned with all the *mys* in my life: my needs, my wants, my goals, my stuff, my desires, my ways . . . *my, my, my* . . .

Thankfully, God tells us in Scripture of a cure for the disease of self-a-holicism. Second Corinthians 9:7 says, "You must each decide in your heart how much to give. And don't give reluctantly or in response to pressure. 'For God loves a person who gives cheerfully'" (NLT).

Notice it doesn't say, "You must each decide in your heart *if you want* to give." No, God says *to give* . . . purposefully, freely, happily. The first step in my self-a-holic recovery was to admit that I had a problem, and that problem was standing in the way of me obeying this verse. That problem was me. Through my recovery, I realized that I had to put all the *mys* in my life on the altar to be sacrificed.

In Genesis 22, God asked Abraham to sacrifice his precious son as an act of utter faith that God would provide. While what God asked me to sacrifice doesn't come anywhere close to comparing to what He asked of Abraham, the principle is the same. It was a matter of the heart. I needed to sacrifice my mys as an act of faith. Little by little, I began doing this by praying about how God wanted me to spend my finances, my time, and my service. And when I felt that familiar nudge, I started obeying right away.

Doing so built my trust that God would take care of my needs. It helped me prioritize my wants. Something shifted in my heart. I thought less of myself and more of others. I found joy in giving my stuff, my time, and my energy away.

I experienced firsthand that God provides—not always in the manner we may have thought of or want, but He's always faithful to give us what we need when we need it.

My kids are now grown, but for years after God asked me to give their clothes to my friend, I did. It became a regular practice for me to buy the clothes, take care of them during the time my children used them, and as the clothes were outgrown, to eagerly look forward to filling the bags for Stacey's children. (After all, my *mys* aren't mine—everything I have belongs to God, and I'm just taking care of it until He asks me to pass it on.) Through continual obedience, this self-a-holic no longer holds onto her stuff with a tight fist, but she gives with a cheerful attitude.

Dear Lord,

Help me to see the needs of others and be willing to
obey You when You call me to sacrifice my mys.
Change my self-a-holic heart to be selfless, like Your heart.

In Jesus's Name, Amen.

NO TO SELF INVITES REVELATION FROM GOD

The 320 Life is a beautiful spiritual waltz with the Holy Spirit and the authority of God's Word as your partners. At the start of your dance, you move joyfully to the rhythm of *yes*. In full disclosure, this dance comes to an abrupt halt when you embark on the next principle: *no* to self.

It's much easier to embrace this next principle of the 320 Life with a friend by your side. I have my group of gal pals, my solid-when-life-spins-out-of-control-and-I-need-help go-to team. If I were about to enter a dangerous situation, any of these godly women would warn me to be cautious. They help me say *no* when my flesh wants to say *yes*. I'm that friend for you.

I'm not going to lie; this phase of the 320 Life is tough. It makes saying *yes* to God seem like riding a bike with training wheels for the first time. There will be times you long for the days you glided across the *yes* dance floor. The wealth of *no* is much more difficult to discover, and your toes will be stepped on in the process. That's because we'll be learning how to say *no* to self in a *yes*-to-self world. I want to encourage you to stand firm in what you've learned so far. Remember, *yes* is the first step to the life you always wanted. Continue to love God with your *yes*, no matter how obnoxiously the world instructs, or how loudly your flesh insists, otherwise.

I'm going to press refresh on our Warren Wiersbe commentary paraphrase on "exceeding abundantly above all that we ask or think" (I threw a little King James in for fun): We get our hands on our spiritual wealth by opening our hearts to God.

Our spiritual wealth is found when we say no to self, because . . .

No to self invites revelation from God.

Something to Pursue

STUDYING AND LEARNING PSALM 119

Of the 27 books in the New Testament, Paul penned almost half of them. He sent his 13 letters to individuals and to churches to teach, inspire, encourage, and correct them. But before Paul wrote these epistles instructing others, he himself needed insight from the Lord. He needed what the psalmist asked for in Psalm 119:34, "Give me understanding, so that I may keep your law and obey it with all my heart" (NIV).

The psalmist wasn't asking to simply know the letter of the law; he already had the head knowledge of God's commandments. Instead, he was seeking spiritual understanding. Paul also had plenty of head knowledge that he'd gained from his years of learning under Gamaliel, a well-respected rabbi in the Jewish Sanhedrin. What Paul needed was spiritual understanding, and he gained it after his encounter with Jesus on the road to Damascus.

Whatever you say no to is a gain, not a loss.

Through that transformation, God gave Paul the spiritual understanding he lacked. This spiritual understanding of God's law—His ways and commands—is knowledge of the Gospel and Christ. This knowledge leads to a love for and commitment to purity and holiness, which leads us to turn away from temptation and sin. One commentary puts it this way: "With my whole heart. — I will not trifle with my God, I will not divide my affections with the world; God shall have all."[1] Or, as our apostle wrote to the church in Philippi: "What is more, I consider everything a loss because of the surpassing worth of knowing Christ Jesus my Lord, for whose sake I have lost all things. I consider them garbage, that I may gain Christ" (Phil. 3:8 [NIV]).

Ask God to give you a love and dedication to His law—His ways. Pray for a deep desire to obey Him with all your heart and to view whatever you say *no* to as a gain, not a loss. Our understanding and commitment to God's law leads us to the 320 Life—a life with more joy, hope, peace, and love than is even imaginable.

Challenge Verse: Psalm 119:34

Highlight and write down your favorite translation of this week's verse on an index card or a piece of paper. Post the card on your mirror where you get ready every day, next to your favorite chair, or by your coffee maker so you can read it frequently. This will help you learn the verse and put it into practice.

- ❖ "Give me understanding and I will obey your instructions; I will put them into practice with all my heart." (NLT)

- ❖ "Give me understanding, so that I may comply with Your Law and keep it with all my heart." (NASB)

- ❖ "Help me understand your teachings, and I will follow them. Obeying them will be my greatest desire." (ERV)

- ❖ "Give me insight so I can do what you tell me—my whole life one long, obedient response." (THE MESSAGE)

IMMEASURABLY MORE STATEMENT

The Immeasurably More Life doesn't come without cost.

Whether you grew up going to church or not, you likely have heard the phrase, "It is more blessed to give than to receive" (Acts 20:35 [NIV]). My friend Cassie learned how true this verse is during a memorable season in her life. With her husband in seminary, they agreed that she'd pick up most of Matt's usual household duties, in addition to her own. On top of his going to graduate school, both worked full time, cared for her mother, and volunteered at church; they were wiped out by the end of the week.

One evening, during dinner at their friends Kate and Pete's house, Pete mentioned how he wanted to study the Bible . . . *really* study the Bible. He wanted to grasp the Greek and Hebrew, learn about contexts and cultures, know the authors and audiences of the books, and understand biblical exegesis and hermeneutics. As Matt and Pete talked, Cassie saw her husband light up. One thing led to another and before Cassie knew it, Matt turned to her and asked, "What do you think if I led a small group here at Pete and Kate's on Friday evenings? Will you pray about it?"

Pray about it? Cassie didn't even want to think about it. She knew that it would take her husband hours each week to prepare for teaching, which meant more duties would be piled higher on her plate. Her first thoughts were: *We already have too much going on. And I'm tired by Friday night. By the end of the week, I just want to put on my pajamas and watch a movie.*

But she did commit to pray, and as she did, her resolved no to the Bible study turned into a resolute *no* to self. Cassie felt God reassure her that when she let go of her concerns and desires, that He'd replenish both her and Matt. She recalled

Acts 20:35, "It is more blessed to give than to receive" (NIV). The Greek word for blessed is *makarion*. Can you guess what it means? Happy. How great is that? What a promise from God.

Despite knowing that promise, Cassie still felt tired that first Friday night they left their house for small group. Even though she'd agreed to it, every bone in her body was weary. But a funny thing happened when everyone gathered together; her tiredness subsided, and she felt excited to be there. Deep diving into Scripture, talking about the Lord, ministering to others, and praying with them renewed her. On the drive home, she and her husband marveled at how much joy God had poured out on them during the evening.

Let's read Acts 20:35 again, this time changing one word: "It is more *happy* to give than to receive." The Immeasurably More Life doesn't come without cost. But when we say *no* to self, even when it costs us precious time and energy, and when we give out of the abundance that God's gifted us with, He fills us with His joy. That is living the 320 Immeasurably More Life!

Something to View

VIDEO LISTENING GUIDE

Headstrong. Stubborn. Strong-willed. Looking back at myself through the lens of Scripture, these are the adjectives I'd use to describe myself, an admission I'm not proud to make. It is apparent to me now; this is why I found the wealth of *no* to self so challenging.

I'm a *same* girl, a creature of habit. Changes are NOT easy for me, so when the Holy Spirit started to stir the *same* girl in a new direction, I was, well—to put it nicely—less than cooperative. You see, I didn't mind change, as long as God was making someone else change and was working things out for my good. Am I alone? Didn't think so.

In time, like me, you will see that the adjustments God wants to make in your life are truly for your good and His glory, to help you resemble your heavenly Father. Yes, the reshaping can be difficult, and it will be costly (*the Immeasurably More Life doesn't come without cost*). But the more you surrender to God's Work and His Word, the more you will realize that the benefits outweigh the cost. You will experience the family resemblance when you forgive the hurt, give without expectation, don't lose your temper, etc. The thrill of seeing Christ's reflection in yourself will be so overwhelming that you will long to see it again and again, no matter the cost.

The secret to obedience and to knowing when to say *no* to self is to recognize when the Holy Spirit is speaking. Much like your best friend that you do everything with and whose voice you know without needing caller ID when she calls, after spending time with the Lord in prayer and in His Word, you will be able to discern and recognize when He is speaking to you. John 10 affirms this: "But the one who enters through the gate is the shepherd of the sheep. The gatekeeper opens the gate for him, and the sheep recognize his voice and come to him. He calls his own sheep by name and leads them out" (vv. 2–3 [NLT]). Jesus goes on to say that His sheep (Believers) will trust and know Him too well to follow a stranger's voice. "They won't follow a stranger; they will run from him because they don't know his voice" (John 10:5 [NLT]).

Knowing that God, our Good Shepherd, is there to speak to us and guide us in saying no to self is a comfort. If you struggle, pray for help. A loving father doesn't mind when his child asks for help. In fact, asking for help gives a father the opportunity to fellowship and interact with his child, to share from his vast wisdom and expansive knowledge. Our heavenly Father reacts to us, His children, the same way. All we have to do is ask for help. Our Something to Pursue verse directs us to ask God for clarity and help: "Help me understand your teachings, and I will follow them. Obeying them will be my greatest desire" (Ps. 119:34 [ERV]). As we study this verse, we will answer two questions:

1. How does God give understanding?

2. How does understanding God's commands cost me?

Question 1: How does God give understanding?

To gain understanding of any subject, it's helpful to have a teacher. God has given us the best one.

"But you have received the _____, and He lives within you, so you don't need anyone to _____ you what is true. For the _____ teaches you _____ you need to know, and what He _____ is true—it is not a lie. So just as He has taught you, remain in fellowship with Christ." 1 John 2:27 (NLT)

Who else do I need to help me understand Scripture? _____

No invites revelation from God, revelation into how we are living and if our lifestyle aligns rightly with the Word of God. Our Teacher teaches us what adjustments we need to make so we can reflect the image we were created to live before sin entered the world. As we submit to the Holy Spirit's work, He not only reveals what needs adjusting, but He will also supply the power to accomplish the work. "For God is working in you, giving you the desire and the power to do what pleases him." Phil. 2:13 (NLT)

Our image was _____ and _____ in Genesis 1:26–27: "Then God said, 'Let us make mankind in our image, in our likeness . . . .' So, God created mankind in his own image, in the image of God he created them; male and female he created them." (NIV)

Lasting lifestyle change is not possible without the conviction of the Holy Spirit and the power of the Holy Scriptures.

Believers are to live _____ fed and _____ led. The Teacher helps with both.

Question 2: How does understanding God's commands cost me?

No one stands up and voluntarily says, "Why, yes, I'd love to be last, give up my spot, say *no* to my dream, and serve you all my favorite things." We are born with ourselves in mind. Serve one Sunday in the two-year-old class in the church nursery and count how many times you hear, "Mine!" *No* transforms us from self-centered to God-centered.

While Louie Giglio uses the more palatable phrase, "i am not" (in his book *i am not, but i know I AM*), Jesus uses less-pleasing verbs, like lose and give up:

> "If you try to hang on to your life, you will lose it. But if you give up your life for my sake and for the sake of the Good News, you will save it." Mark 8:35 (NLT)

In God's economy, the _____ is the winner.

Loser to winner definitions:

_____: to put out of the way entirely, abolish, put an end to, ruin, render useless.

_____: the vital force that animates our body for Him.

_____: properly, *deliver* out of danger and *into safety*; used principally of God *rescuing* believers *from* the penalty and power of sin—*and into His provisions (safety).*

The Immeasurably More Life doesn't _____ without _____, but it is worth the price you pay.

At this point we've got to determine that our _____ to know Christ has to be greater than our concern over our hurt feelings.

> *"We must allow the Word of God to correct us*
> *the same way we allow it to encourage us."*
>
> —A.W. Tozer

Devotion

RESHAPING ME

"Since we are living by the Spirit, let us follow the Spirit's leading in every part of our lives." Gal. 5:25 (NLT)

Others might find their simple pleasures in sunny spring days on the porch, cool fall evenings with the family toasting marshmallows, or the company of a good friend. Me? One of my favorite pleasures is haircut day.

Driving to the salon, I smiled thinking about how much I would enjoy the pampering experience. Little did I know that God had a more important experience waiting for me. I had plans to have my unruly mop reshaped, while God had plans to reshape my character. After my cut, style, and primping time, I grabbed my purse to pay for my new 'do. "Before I go," I said to my stylist, "I need to use your bathroom."

Walking in, I immediately noticed the dirty ring around the toilet bowl, the soap scum buildup in the sink, and, well . . . the gross things that form around the base of the commode. Disgusted, I began to criticize and question the salon's sanitation regulations. In the midst of my harsh judgements, I sensed the Holy Spirit whisper something to me that I didn't want to hear.

No. You can't be serious, I argued.

Again, I heard His whisper. Again, I debated. I found myself teetering. Would I follow the Holy Spirit's direction or flush, wash, and leave?

Frozen, I was unable to move toward the door. My only option was to yield. I looked around at the various cleaning products, took a deep breath, grabbed a handful of paper towels and a worn-out toilet brush, and I began to obey the Spirit's direction.

At first, I wasn't thrilled or interested in doing a good job. My goal was to hurry up and get out. But while on my hands and knees, scrubbing and wiping, God's reshaping of my character continued as I heard the whisper, *"As you would your own."*

It wasn't enough that I had yielded; God wanted my heart to be right. So I cleaned with greater fervor, as if it were my own bathroom. Galatians 5:25 reminds us that we don't live according to what the world tells us. Or what our stubborn will tells us. Scripture tells us that we live by the Spirit, which means saying *yes* to God and *no* to self. When we do this, it's much easier to "follow the Spirit's leading in every part of our lives" (Gal. 5:25 [NLT]).

As I worked to change the bathroom, the Lord changed me. My pride turned to humility as I thought about the next person who would enter the restroom. Envisioning the look on her face as she smelled the fresh, clean aroma and saw sparkling chrome brought me great joy. This joy melted away my stubbornness as I experienced God's delight.

Today, tomorrow, or in the future, you will be given the opportunity to follow the Holy Spirit's leading, as Galatians 5:25 tells us to do. Maybe you will not be asked to clean a public bathroom, but there is no doubt your choice to seize or ignore whatever opportunity God presents to you will reshape your character. How will you respond?

Dear Lord,

Thank You for the opportunity to know You as Savior and Lord.
Today and each day forward, I want to seize every chance I have to be more like You.
Forgive me for ignoring opportunities in the past.
Thank You for wanting to reshape my character.

In Jesus's Name, Amen.

STUDY QUESTIONS

No to self is where the rubber meets the road in our relationship with Christ. The 320 Life has nothing to do with salvation. When you are saved, you can't get more saved or become less saved. The no-to-self phase builds upon your relationship with Christ; as you say no to self, you start to be more like Him. This is the gateway to living the superabundant life with our Immeasurably More God. We do this with gratitude for the generous and undeserved gift of salvation, which motivates us to serve others selflessly.

1. Inviting revelation begins with praying King David's prayer of investigation by God into our heart, mind, and character (we began praying this prayer in Psalm 139 in week one). Praying this prayer requires courage; yes, courage. Once you begin praying this way, you can't unpray it. The Holy Spirit will begin to mess with your beautiful, your contentment, and your life as you know it. Don't let this scare you off or make you hesitant though. I promise, it all turns out well for the person who loves God and is called according to His purpose: "And we know that God causes everything to work together for the good of those who love God and are called according to his purpose for them" (Rom. 8:28 [NLT]).

    Turn to Psalm 139:23–24. In the space provided, write these verses. For fun, you can use an online website or Bible app to look up different translations (like Bible Hub, BibleGateway, or YouVersion). My personal favorite translation is *The Message* by Eugene Peterson.

Begin to pray this prayer every day. Perhaps even write the prayer on an index card and keep it in your Bible (this is what I did).

2. How do you feel about being corrected by God? I'm not speaking only of correction regarding your spiritual life.

3. The Bible has much to say about correction/discipline. Some of it is pleasant and palatable, but some of it . . . not so much. Hang in there with me.

   What words are used to describe the discipline/correction in Hebrews 12:11? (Put a bookmark in your Bible; we'll revisit this verse in just a minute.)

   What occurs in the life of the person who accepts discipline/correction?

   Solomon, the wisest king to have ever ruled, has some strong language about the person who disregards correction. Brace yourself; I wouldn't let my children use this kind of language when they were young. We called it the "S" word. Turn to Proverbs 12:1 and write the verse in the space below.

   Now the good news! Who does God discipline/correct? Quick, turn again to the good news in Hebrews 12:11 and write the verse in the space below.

4. We can't only accept the positive from God and not endure the polishing also. Remember, the Holy Spirit helps us reshape our image. We were made in the image of God, "So God created man in his own image, in the image of God he created him; male and female he created them" (Gen. 1:27 [ESV]). Regarding the statements below, which one is your typical response when receiving revelation from God? Circle your answer and write to the Lord the reason you made the choice you did.

- ⭕ I ignore what God has revealed, because I really want to do what I want to do. I'm okay with a mediocre relationship with Christ—that's enough for me.
- ⭕ I condemn myself and reject what God reveals, because I can't leave my past behind and don't believe I'm worthy.
- ⭕ I reply in humility and accept what God reveals, because I long to be like Christ and am willing to do what it takes.

....

....

....

5. Change isn't easy or popular. Our world tells us to look out for ourselves, but God says to surrender ourselves. His Word empowers us to do what the world says we can't. "For the Spirit God gave us does not make us timid, but gives us power, love and self-discipline" (2 Tim. 1:7 [NIV]). Let's spend some time exploring three ways our no-to-self phase can be easily disrupted, and how God has provided all we need to stay centered on Him.

❖ Strongholds and Power

In Scripture, a stronghold is an argument or reasoning that one believes and finds shelter in. These can be false arguments or true arguments. God's Word provides positive, hopeful, and life-changing strongholds. Our enemy, Satan, does everything in his power to deny God's truths by reminding us of our past failures and fears. "For though we walk in the flesh, we are not waging war according to the flesh. For the weapons of our warfare are not of the flesh but have divine power to destroy strongholds" (2 Cor. 10:3–4 [ESV]). Hallelujah, God gives us power to defeat strongholds. "[Inasmuch as we] refute arguments and theories and reasonings and every proud and lofty thing that sets itself up against the [true] knowledge of God; and we lead every thought and purpose away captive into the obedience of Christ (the Messiah, the Anointed One)" (2 Cor. 10:5 [AMPC]).

What false strongholds have gripped your life? Rely on God's power to help you defeat any strongholds that have a hold on you.

....

....

What positive strongholds have gripped your life?

....

....

✤ Self-centeredness and Love

A person who cares only about their own wants and interests is self-centered. I believe we can all agree this is the exact opposite of a life devoted to God. God's love not only has the power to save a life, but it is also long-suffering and powerful enough to transform a life. Again, we shout, "Hallelujah!" Without God's unfailing love and infallible truth, and the Holy Spirit's tireless efforts, we would remain in our born image: self-centered. "So we have come to know and to believe the love that God has for us. God is love, and whoever abides in love abides in God, and God abides in him" (1 John 4:16 [ESV]). Abiding in this kind of perfect love provides us with the confidence and peace we need to allow God's Word to do its work in our life.

What areas of self-centeredness in your life need God's patient, transformational love?

....

....

....

✤ Self-sufficiency and Power

One of the many false narratives the world has scripted for us is "you are capable of taking care of yourself." Unfortunately, this is a trap we fall into easily.

All sources of media paint the picture of success as someone who has a higher education, is in a position of authority, dines at expensive restaurants, lives in a big house, and drives a luxury car. None of these are wrong. However, we can't fall for the lie that we accomplish, obtain, or maintain anything apart from God. "I am the Vine; you are the branches. Whoever lives in Me and I in him bears much (abundant) fruit. However, apart from Me [cut off from vital union with Me] you can do nothing" (John 15:5 [AMPC]). When we find ourselves feeling puffed up by our accomplishments and relying on our material wealth and positions, we are flirting with self-sufficiency. The power to break this cycle is found in God's Word. Self-discipline is a gift from God. He gives the gift and the power to succeed. Let's revisit 2 Timothy 1:7 in another translation, "For God has not given us a spirit of fear and timidity, but of power, love, and self-discipline" (NLT). Grab your pen and circle the word *given*. We can't use or enjoy a gift unless we open it.

What areas of self-sufficiency in your life need self-discipline? What is the first step you will take?

....

....

6. The secret to the success in this phase is something we mentioned earlier—losing our life for Christ's sake. Jesus talked a lot in the gospels about the mystifying concept of losing and finding life. Look up the following references and write the verses in the spaces below.

John 12:25

....

....

Matthew 16:25

....

....

How do these verses challenge you?

....

....

7. As we find the beautiful rhythm of *yes* to God and *no* to self, the internal work of the Spirit in us will be noticed externally. How will our life reveal God's work? See Galatians 5:22–23.

_____

_____

_____

_____

_____

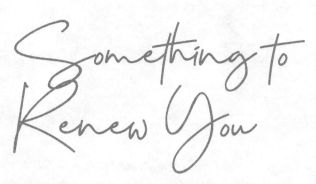

JOURNAL ENTRY BETWEEN YOU AND JESUS

Use this space to journal what you hear from the Lord in your time of prayer and what you learn as you study God's Word. It may be that you offer God adoration, praise, thanks, or repentance. Or it may be that God offers you encouragement, direction, correction, or healing. Don't worry about punctuation, grammar, or spelling; just write. It's all between you and Jesus.

Devotion

FRESHEN UP

"He lets me rest in green meadows; He leads me beside peaceful streams. He renews my strength. He guides me along right paths, bringing honor to his name." Ps. 23:2–3 (NLT)

A few summers ago, as I washed the dinner dishes in my hot kitchen, I noticed my house plants were suffering from the effects of a drought—a drought my black thumb had caused indoors. My heart saddened as I looked at the shriveled leaves on my beautiful peace lily. I quickly filled one of the cups I was cleaning and watered my pitiful plants.

Over the next few weeks, I kept a close eye on them and tended to them often with fresh water. Much to my relief, the leaves started to revive and reach up and out to me, as if to say, "Thank you for the drink." Then one day I noticed a bloom opening! All of this renewed growth and new fruit was simply from regular watering. God quickly reminded me, "You need water too. No water, no fruit." I knew just what He meant.

Oftentimes in the long days of summer, I can become like my wilted lily. With the kids out of school, vacations, home projects, and cookouts with friends, I can quickly neglect my daily time with God. My Bible gathers many layers of dust between readings. And my prayer life runs dry. Simply put, I am in a spiritual drought because I don't drink from God's Word or restore my soul with His presence.

Psalm 23 tells us that the Lord—our good Shepherd—will lead us, His sheep, to refreshing and still streams of water in the midst of lush pastures. "He makes me lie down in green pastures, he leads me beside quiet waters, he refreshes my soul" (vv. 1–3 [NIV]). Sheep are generally timid, afraid of rushing and loud rivers, so their shepherd will guide them to still, cool places to drink and eat—to be restored in the heat of the day. The key, however, is that the sheep have to follow their shepherd to the source of water. If they don't, they will become parched and dehydrated in the noonday sun.

When life gets busy, we get distracted and can forget (or neglect) to follow our Shepherd to refreshing waters. We don't drink daily from His Word or renew ourselves with prayer. Can you relate? Many churches don't offer weekly Bible studies or small groups in the summer because of how busy people get with various activities. Some pastors even take a summer sabbatical and have guest preachers in their place. This often leads to people skipping church services over the summer months until their pastor returns.

Between home life, work life, and church life all being less structured, it's so easy for us to take the summer off from spending quality time with the Lord and in His Word. Let me caution you to determine not to take the summer—or any season— off, whether it be a season of life, a season of hardship, or a season of busyness.

If having a structured study is helpful for you, do something new with something old. Here are some ideas for you to try:

- Pull out a previously completed Bible Study and read your notes.

- Pour over your Sunday school lessons from the last year.

- Take a fresh look at scriptures your pastor taught on in his sermons by studying commentaries on them.

- Look up your favorite Bible verses in various translations. Nothing makes Scripture come alive for me—outside of the Holy Spirit's power—than reading the ancient words in other translations.

Whatever you choose to do, stick with it! Make a commitment for the next 365 days to water your relationship with God daily through prayer and Bible reading. If necessary, plan now for what you will study during the next season of your life, so you don't find yourself in a spiritual drought in the midst of it. Your Good Shepherd will refresh your soul.

Dear Lord,

Lead me to the refreshing living water of Your Word every day, in every season. I pray that I will delight myself in You, and that You will enjoy my company.

In Jesus's Name, Amen.

Week 4

THE WEALTH
OF *MAYBE*

The Immeasurably More Life
isn't rushed; it's relaxed.

Devotion

A MARY MOMENT

"Blessed are you among women, and blessed is the child you will bear! But why am I so favored, that the mother of my Lord should come to me? . . . Blessed is she who has believed that the Lord would fulfill his promises to her!" Luke 1:42–43, 45 (NIV)

I love the story of Jesus's mother Mary—young, sweet, innocent Mary—who accepted the assignment of her lifetime when the angel Gabriel announced she would give birth to the Son of the Most High. Can you imagine what she was thinking as he told her how her *son* would be conceived, who Jesus would be, and that He would reign forever? Though troubled at first, once Mary heard all the angel had been sent to tell her, she responded with faith and obedience: "May it happen to me as you have said" (Luke 1:38 [GNT]).

After receiving this news, Mary did what most women do when something "big" happens—she ran to tell a trusted friend, her cousin Elizabeth. Perhaps she needed comfort or wisdom from someone older. Maybe she wanted to share her excitement. Or possibly she needed a reassuring hug from someone who loved her. Whatever her reasoning, Mary hurried to Zechariah and Elizabeth's house.

When she arrived at their home, Mary received confirmation that God had indeed chosen her to give birth to the long-awaited Messiah. Upon seeing Mary, Elizabeth exclaimed, "Blessed are you among women, and blessed is the child you will bear! But why am I so favored, that the mother of my Lord should come to me? . . . Blessed is she who has believed that the Lord would fulfill his promises to her" (Luke 1:42–43, 45 [NIV])!

This was Mary's moment. All that she had believed of what the angel had spoken was affirmed. In response, Mary praised God, saying, "My soul glorifies the Lord and my spirit rejoices in God my Savior, for he has been mindful of the humble state of his servant. From now on all generations will call me blessed, for the Mighty One has done great things for me—holy is his name" (Luke 1:46–49 [NIV]).

What an amazing assignment from God and a remarkable response from Mary! God gave other people in Scripture assignments of a lifetime too; they proved to also be faithful and obedient. He trusted the woman at the well to tell others about Him, even though she was an outcast. He called Rahab to be brave and hide the Israelite spies, even though she risked being caught. He asked Esther to seek the favor of the king, even though she and her people could have all perished. He asked Martha to be still and rest in His presence, even though she had guests to tend to.

Is God speaking to you today about accepting a divine assignment? It may not be as radical as Mary or Esther's assignments, but it is special enough that God is appointing it to you. Maybe He wants you to share His Word with others, to financially support missions or to become a missionary, or to press pause on whatever keeps you too busy to be with Him. Has the Lord been speaking to you through His Word and prayer? Have you been sensing Him telling you something that seems outrageous? Has He asked you to say "yes" or "no" to something life-changing?

I know at first it may be bewildering for a couple of days. You probably are wondering if you really heard right. You may be replaying the scenario in your mind to get a clearer picture of the experience, but you still cannot get a handle on it.

Give it time. If it is from the Lord, He will send confirmation. God may use a pastor, scripture, song, friend, family member, or situation to confirm what He has spoken to your heart. Maybe this devotion is confirmation of your own "Mary moment." If so, like Mary, will you respond with a song of praise to the Lord?

Or maybe you are still waiting on your lifetime assignment. God gives each assignment in His perfect timing. Stay close to Him and His Word so when He speaks, you'll be ready to say "yes" and to respond like Mary by saying, "May it happen to me as you have said" (Luke 1:38 [GNT]).

Dear Lord,

Thank You for the assignments You've already given me.
I celebrate with You the future assignments You have for me.
With a willing heart, I wait on the next one.
Thank You for choosing me to be part of Your story.

In Jesus's Name, Amen.

The Wealth of Maybe

MAYBE WELCOMES FREEDOM WITH GOD

When I was a child, the one word my parents said the most that I liked the least was *maybe*. You see, I was an energetic, inquisitive child, who always wanted something to do or somewhere to go. If my parents were busy when I bugged them, they wouldn't offer me a definitive *yes* or *no* answer. They'd simply say, "Maybe, Wendy." It wasn't until my son was born that I truly appreciated the toil they endured by my young self. It was through raising my own kids that I learned the power—as well as the freedom—that the word *maybe* welcomes.

Maybe has power. This small word inserts a pause into any situation, question, or opportunity. It carries enough weight to influence the outcome of a critical, or even a trivial, decision. The word *maybe* is invaluable to the believer living the 320 Life. It welcomes flexibility and insists on stepping back from an invitation to take the time to seek the wisdom necessary for the best outcome. In a word, *maybe* is freedom.

Freedom doesn't come without cost. In the previous weeks, we've studied at great length what is necessary for Christ followers to live the life He died to give. The price that Christ paid on Calvary offers us life beyond death, eternity with Him and our Father God. But the price we pay to live the abundant, full, and free life while we are here on earth—our *yeses* and our *nos*—ushers us to a place of freedom that enhances the price Christ paid on the cross.

Maybe is the sugar in the tea, the icing on the cake, and the surprise ninth chicken nugget in your eight-count box. The seasons and cycles of learning *yes* and *no* have ushered you to the life you always wanted and wondered how to have—the life Jesus died to give you. He said it best, "The thief comes only in order to steal and kill and destroy. I came that they may have *and* enjoy life, and have it in abundance (to the full, till it overflows)" (John 10:10 [AMPC], emphasis added). This life of immeasurably more, of abundance, that is full and overflows with joy, is experienced when our life intersects and is surrendered to God's ways. Its freedom is summarized beautifully in our Something to Pursue verse of the week.

Once more, let's wrap our minds around the wonderfully powerful words of how God "is able to [carry out His purpose and] do superabundantly, far over and above all that we [dare] ask or think [infinitely beyond our highest prayers, desires, thoughts, hopes, or dreams]" (Eph. 3:20 [AMPC]). To paraphrase Mr. Wiersbe one final time: *We get our hands on our spiritual wealth by opening our hearts to God.*

Our spiritual wealth is found when we say maybe to others . . .
because maybe welcomes freedom with God.

Something to Pursue

STUDYING AND LEARNING PSALM 119

It's hard to imagine someone who endured more for the sake of Christ than the apostle Paul. He suffered imprisonment, beatings, lashings, and being stoned over and over. Paul shipwrecked not once, not twice, but three times! Dangerous people continually hunted him, so they could persecute him. He often went without food, drink, and sleep. And if all that was not enough, Paul carried the weight of the care and concern he felt for the churches and people that he loved.

You would think that being hunted down would cause Paul to be so fearful that he would stop preaching in public, but he continued to boldly proclaim the Gospel. It's almost shocking that he didn't go into hiding after being beaten multiple times. Yet the apostle continued to travel, declaring Christ's salvation. And would you blame him if he'd have questioned why God had allowed so much hardship to come his way? But as far as Scripture reveals, Paul stayed steadfast throughout his life. How? Perhaps because he understood the freedom—freedom from fear, freedom from doubt, freedom from hopelessness—that is found only in obeying God's Word: "I will walk about in freedom, for I have sought out your precepts" (Ps. 119:45 [NIV]).

> *Freedom from fear, freedom from doubt, freedom from hopelessness—that is found only in obeying God's Word.*

The psalmist here declared "that what he would willingly do by the grace of God, and strives to do, is to walk . . . in a broad space . . . courageously and unconstrainedly, without allowing myself to be intimidated, and said of inward freedom which makes itself known outwardly." Despite all of Paul's turmoil and the thousands of reasons he had to be fearful and hesitant to continue to walk in God's ways, he followed them with steely resolve. He laid aside any hindrances, doubts, sins, and worldly desires and God replaced them with boldness, peace, joy, and a desire to obey God's precepts.

Paul and the psalmist understood that "they who simply walk after God's word have no nets to entangle them, while they who do contrary are ever in nets and snares." As you and I come to fully understand and embrace that knowledge too, we'll move further into living the life we always wanted. We'll know when to say yes, no, and maybe with confidence. That's living the 320 Life, that proclaims: "Now all glory to God, who is able, through his mighty power at work within us, to accomplish infinitely more than we might ask or think" (Eph. 3:20 [NLT]).

Challenge Verse: Psalm 119:45

Highlight and write down your favorite translation of this week's verse on an index card or a piece of paper. Post the card on your mirror where you get ready every day, next to your favorite chair, or by your coffee maker so you can read it frequently. This will help you learn the verse and put it into practice.

- ❖ "I will walk in freedom, for I have devoted myself to your commandments." (NLT)

- ❖ "And I will walk at liberty *and* at ease, for I have sought and inquired for [and desperately required] Your precepts." (AMP)

- ❖ "I have gained perfect freedom by following your teachings." (CEV)

- ❖ "Therefore, I will keep on obeying you forever and forever, free within the limits of your laws." (TLB)

Something to Hold Onto

IMMEASURABLY MORE STATEMENT

The Immeasurably More Life isn't rushed; it's relaxed—
relaxed in a confident faith in God.

We are devoted to many things: family, church, profession, community, hobbies, and good health, just to name a few. Our devotion to these and other things isn't wrong, unless or until they become a distraction from true devotion to God. We can be so devoted to serving God that we are more devoted to *serving* rather than to the God whom we serve. Being this busy and overscheduled can be dangerous; so, it's important to select our places of service well.

This reminds me of an older gentleman at my church and his one act of service that blessed the whole congregation every single week. Each Sunday, my husband and I would usher our children into the main sanctuary for the church service. We'd take our seats in the same pew in the balcony. And each week they would be there, sharpened with a perfect point, ready to use: the yellow pencils.

I never thought much about the flawlessly honed writing utensils until I happened to be at the church office one Tuesday morning. A dapper older gentleman brushed by with a box of pencils in one hand and a sharpener in the other. My mind flashed back to the pencils in the pews. With a bent brow, I asked someone, "Is he the one who sharpens the pew pencils?" Sure enough, he was the mystery man.

Each week, this man quietly eased in and out, with few taking notice. Sharpening the pencils was his way of serving the Lord. Now, he was retired and his children were grown, so you could argue that he had time to serve in a million more ways. But this was the act of service that God had called this man to in this season of his life. He didn't need to be part of every committee, board, or league. Week after week, he simply needed to faithfully perform his one act of service. In doing so, this humble servant was living out Colossians 3:17, "And whatever you do, in word or deed, do everything in the name of the Lord Jesus, giving thanks to God the Father through him" (ESV).

Maybe God is calling you to do only one thing in this season of your life. That will mean saying *yes* to that one thing, *no* to different tasks, and *maybe* to other opportunities. Pray and ask the Lord where He'd have you serve. No matter how big or small it may seem . . . no matter how much or little time it takes . . . accept your assignment, remembering that the Immeasurably More Life isn't rushed; it's relaxed—relaxed in a confident faith in God.

I love what John Stephen has to say about Psalm 119:45: "To what expansion of mind does a man awake when he becomes conscious of being in the appointed way of God! And he is actually at liberty; for the good providence of God is around him, and his grace supports him." A believer truly devoted to God deliberates before deciding, and only someone who is walking fully in the 320 Life knows the freedom that comes with every *yes*, *no*, and *maybe*.

Something to View

VIDEO LISTENING GUIDE

Have you ever had a parking lot conversion? Let me explain. You are the lead teacher for the children's four-year-old Sunday school class, the coordinator for the Lord's Supper, the towel-bringer for baptisms, and the soloist for the choir anthem. I sense anxiety rising. Let me guess . . . you've been there. I'll continue.

You get up at zero dark thirty to make sure everything goes as planned. You are dressed and ready and have breakfast on the table by the time your family members stumble out of bed. The baby throws up on you, the four year old doesn't like the outfit you selected for him to wear, and your spouse gets called into work. I'll continue.

Angry that you are going to church alone, you hustle the kids and all the bags into the minivan, rush down the road, and skid into the church parking lot on two wheels. Hopping out of the van, you grab the kids and aggressively slam the doors, all the while mumbling less-than-nice things under your breath. Suddenly, you spot the pastor crossing the road. You wave with your barely free hand and spout out, "Wonderful Sabbath, isn't it, Pastor? I prayed for you today." Do I need to continue?

You just had a parking lot conversion. (This story is inspired by actual events.)

In this story, serving sounds rushed; in God's plan, serving is relaxed. Serving where and when God designs leads to our service being a place of rest. It leads us to be comfortable pressing pause and saying *maybe* when opportunities present themselves.

The wealth of *maybe* is so lavish, we want to live it well. In order to live maybe well, we have to respond to the what-ifs.

The Immeasurably More Life isn't rushed; it's relaxed—relaxed in a confident faith in God.

Relaxed, confident faith in God is developed with every _____ and _____ .

How do I determine the right service?

Recognize

- ❖ My _____ . You know the voice of the one you spend time with.

- ❖ My _____ . You have one or maybe more gifts, and you may or may not use them.

- ❖ My _____ . Your people and schedule matter.

- ❖ My _____ . God will use your limits to grow you and His Kingdom.

Even when I rightly recognize all the above, things may still go wrong. _____ might interrupt and make me second guess my _____ .

What if my:

- ❖ personal situation changes drastically?

- ❖ place of service turns out to be unlikeable?

- ❖ position isn't what I thought it was going to be?

- ❖ prayed-through decision was the wrong one?

- ❖ perfect decision is awesome, but I sense God leading me on a new adventure?

- ❖ perfect decision turns out to be a huge blessing?

Naturally, even when we are confident that making our *maybe* a *yes* is the right decision, sometimes the what-ifs can't be _____ .

The proper response to every what-if is the same. Make every effort to
....

- ❖ Remember your place of service is to the ....

- ❖ "Work willingly at whatever you do, as though you were working for the Lord rather than for people." Col. 3:23 (NLT)

- ❖ Even if it gets ...., don't stop doing good. "So let's not get tired of doing what is good. At just the right time we will reap a harvest of blessing if we don't give up." Gal. 6:9 (NLT)

- ❖ Everything you do for the Lord is .... "So, my dear brothers and sisters, be strong and immovable. Always work enthusiastically for the Lord, for you know that nothing you do for the Lord is ever useless." 1 Cor. 15:58 (NLT)

- ❖ Serve with .... "Do everything without complaining and arguing." Phil. 2:14 (NLT)

The apostle Paul was radically saved and knew full well what the freedom of living with the God of Immeasurably More was like. He wrote about this freedom in his second letter to the church in Corinth.

"Now the Lord is the Spirit, and where the Spirit of the Lord is, there is freedom."

2 Cor. 3:17 (NIV)

Because we opened our hearts to the wealth of heaven, we live in this same freedom. Freedom:

- ❖ from former blindness and darkness.

- ❖ from the bondage of sin and the captivity of Satan.

- ❖ from the fear of hell, wrath, and damnation.

- ❖ to access God with boldness.

"The highest form of worship is the worship of unselfish Christian service."

—Billy Graham

GET SOME REST

"Come with me by yourselves to a quiet place and get some rest."

Mark 6:31 (NIV)

A while back, my family and I went through a long season where every day had me running around in circles. Early in the year, my mom was diagnosed with cancer. As she rested, sick in the hospital bed, life became overwhelming for me. I provided care of my daddy and my mother-in-law, managed my home and family, and completed ministry assignments, all while helping my mom finish well.

My calendar overflowed with four different schedules and my brain was crammed full of all the decisions I had to make on their behalf. Between grocery shopping and housekeeping for my dad, choosing a nursing home and moving my mother-in-law into it, researching treatments and therapies for my mom, organizing and paying their bills, plus, dealing with my own life—I was exhausted.

I am honored and thankful I had the ability to take care of my parents and mother-in-law, but all the extenuating circumstances was like having a second full-time job. As I sat in a doctor's office during another frenzied day, I scrolled through Facebook. As I looked at my feed, a photo of a friend's vacation stopped me in my tracks. I could almost feel the warm sun and hear the clear water lapping the shore.

My mind rested and shoulders relaxed for just a moment before the physician came in, and I was off again. But I tucked the picture of the beach in the back of my mind, making a mental note that I needed to rest and to spend time with Jesus— very soon.

Does taking time off sound foreign to you? I struggled with it too. With so much to do, I worried that if I took even an hour off, too many balls would drop. But going 24/7 had left me tired, overworked, disorganized, inefficient, and sleep-deprived (not to mention grumpy!). If I was going to get everything on my plate done—and done well—I needed to rest.

In Mark 6, we see a group of guys in desperate need of downtime. The disciples had just returned from ministering in various towns, where they had travelled, preached, healed the sick, and drove out demons. As you can imagine, they were exhausted by the time they came back together. All they wanted to do was sit with Jesus and tell him about their trip.

But the crowds made this nearly impossible. ". . . So many people were coming and going that they did not even have a chance to eat." So, Jesus offered the disciples a beautiful invitation: "Come with me by yourselves to a quiet place and get some rest" (Mark 6:31 [NIV]).

Can you even imagine Jesus inviting you to get away from it all and just relax together? The reality is, His offer stands each and every moment of the day for you and me. But in our go-go-go society, many of us are so busy we don't hear Him beckon us to go with Him to get some rest. With family to care for, bills to pay, broken things to fix, and work deadlines to meet, it's difficult to give ourselves permission to slow down.

But pausing helps to clear our hearts and minds. Quieting our life and really resting—even if only for an hour—enables us to reset our mood and perspective.

Rest may look different for you than it does for me. Maybe you like to enjoy a catnap, tinker with a hobby, plant flowers, take a walk . . . whatever is restful for you, do it. Spend that time with Jesus, just talking to Him about what you're going through and listening for His wisdom. Taking time to rest aligns our perspective with God's and helps us prioritize our tasks (which will still be there when we return to work).

In the midst of caring for my parents and managing three households, I had to get away with Jesus and rest in Him regularly. Taking that time off actually made me more efficient. My mind was clearer to make better decisions, my body was more agile to lift walkers and wheelchairs, and my heart was more gracious to tend to everyone's needs.

Accept Jesus's invitation to spend time with Him in a quiet place. Accept His gift of rest. Mark your calendar now and set time aside for praise and prayer, Scripture reading and silence, naps and knitting (or whatever is restful for you). I think you'll be amazed at how much it refreshes your mind, body, and heart.

Dear Lord,

It seems like I rarely press pause.

Thank You for this reminder to set aside time to rest and to be with You.

In Jesus's Name, Amen.

STUDY QUESTIONS

1. To the casual observer, *maybe* feels indeterminate and uncertain. Discuss your thoughts about living in *maybe*.

   ....

   ....

2. Generosity isn't always about opening our wallet. On many occasions, an investment of time and talents is just as generous as a gift of money. What does living generously mean to you?

   ....

   ....

   ....

3. Freedom with God brings great joy and peace, but it also requires radical living, giving, and loving. How ready are you to welcome freedom with God?

   ....

   ....

   ....

4. What changes will you implement to start living the 320 Life?

   ....

   ....

The wealth of *maybe*, the spiritual wealth we've obtained as we've opened our heart to God through His Word, will help us respond rightly to the what-ifs.

Our focus on Psalm 119 continues. You will find God's Word is more reliable than any self-help book, podcast, Google search, or even your best friend when it comes to making decisions. His Word never fades or fails. The Word is alive, active, and always relevant.

Look up each scripture that is listed below. In the space provided, write how God's Word will help us in our seasons of maybe.

Psalm 119:105

Psalm 119:59

Psalm 119:98

Psalm 119:133

Use the following scriptures to discover three people who finished well. Name the person, and, in your own words, summarize the person's life, including how they demonstrated finishing well.

Person 1
Numbers 20:7–12; Numbers 20:27; Deuteronomy 34:4–7

Who finished well? ....

Person 2
Matthew 4:18–19; Matthew 16:18; Mark 14:67–72; John 21:15–19; Acts 2:38; John 21:18–19

Who finished well? ....

Person 3
Luke 8:1–3; John 20:11–18; Acts 1:14

Who finished well? ....

Something to Renew You

JOURNAL ENTRY BETWEEN YOU AND JESUS

Use this space to journal what you hear from the Lord in your time of prayer and what you learn as you study God's Word. It may be that you offer God adoration, praise, thanks, or repentance. Or it may be that God offers you encouragement, direction, correction, or healing. Don't worry about punctuation, grammar, or spelling; just write. It's all between you and Jesus.

Devotion

STUNNED BY GOD

"He answered, 'I tell you, if these were silent, the very stones would cry out.'" Luke 19:40 (ESV)

Our Bible study leader posed a question that I didn't even have to think about before answering. She asked the group, "When was the last time God stunned you by something He did for you?" I piped up immediately and without hesitation. "Every day. Every day I am stunned that God created me as I am, that He loves me like He does, and that He gives me the blessings that I have."

The blessings God gives me every day really and truly do stun me. I know the word *stun* may sound like an exaggeration. After all, it means to overcome with astonishment. Someone glancing over my life may not be bowled over by what they see. I am not a woman of great wealth or high social standing. I don't possess an Ivy League education or have vast intelligence. My home isn't filled with an abundance of material possessions. From the outside looking in, my life isn't what others might call stunning. But I see it differently.

I may occasionally forget why I walk into a room, but I wake up every day with a mind that is able to articulate thanks to God. I may struggle with fear at times, but I know every day that God is sovereign and in control. My house is 40 years old, but it's cool in the summer and warm in the winter. My body is aging, but I'm healthy enough to walk to the mailbox. My family and I may get on each other's nerves sometimes, but we love one other deeply. And while many of my outfits are thrifted, my food is simple, and my car isn't new . . . I have clothes in my closet, meals on my table, and transportation in my driveway that gets me around town and home again.

Yes, I am stunned by God and all the blessings He's given me. Every moment of every day is an opportunity to be amazed by God and to praise Him for all He does for me. How about you? Are you ever stunned by God? Does His goodness to you—in the momentous and in the mundane—take you by surprise, so much so that you simply have to sing?

In Luke 19, there was a group of people who were overcome with the need to worship. The scene opens with Jesus riding into the city on a colt. The crowd was so elated, they began to praise Him on the spot. "As he was drawing near—already on the way down the Mount of Olives—the whole multitude of his disciples began to rejoice and praise God with a loud voice for all the mighty works that they had seen, saying, 'Blessed is the King who comes in the name of the Lord! Peace in heaven and glory in the highest'" (vv. 37–38 [ESV])!

Of course, this upset some of the religious leaders there, who wanted the people to be quiet immediately. "And some of the Pharisees in the crowd said to him, 'Teacher, rebuke your disciples'" (v. 39 [ESV]). Check out Jesus's reply to them: "I tell you, if these were silent, the very stones would cry out" (v. 40 [ESV]).

This may seem like a funny expression to us now, but "in saying that the stones will cry out, Jesus indicates that the people's acclamations should be encouraged, not suppressed. The people of Jerusalem are expressing great joy, and that joy is so appropriate, so necessary, that, if they did not express praise, it would be appropriate for inanimate objects to fill the void."

Have you ever had such great joy over God—such elation that He is so worthy of praise—that if you didn't worship Him, you felt that the very rocks would cry out? When I look at all my blessings He's given me, this is how I feel. And I found the perfect song to express that joyful praise.

Years ago, on my morning commute, a worship song came on the radio that I had never paid much attention to. As I listened to the words, I began to weep. This song captured my sentiments exactly of when God stuns me, and I need to praise Him! I wanted to lift my hands and face to Him at that very moment, but I thought better of it as I navigated traffic. Once I parked my car, I raised my hands and voice to God in great joy and admiration.

I'll leave the lyrics below to the song that I heard that day, but first I'd love to encourage you to count your blessings from God. Start with something you may have never thought about, like eyesight, soft sheets, or the sun shining. Thank Him for every tangible and intangible thing, for His presence, His Son and Spirit—for everything! Before you know it, you'll be stunned by all the blessings God's given you.

How Can I Keep from Singing

There is an endless song
Echoes in my soul
I hear the music ring
And though the storms may come
I am holding on
To the rock I cling

How can I keep from singing Your praise
How can I ever say enough
How amazing is Your love
How can I keep from shouting Your name
I know I am loved by the King
And it makes my heart want to sing

I will lift my eyes
In the darkest night
For I know my Savior lives

And I will walk with You
Knowing You'll see me through
And sing the songs You give

I can sing in the troubled times
Sing when I win
I can sing when I lose my step
And fall down again
I can sing 'cause You pick me up
Sing 'cause You're there
I can sing 'cause You hear me, Lord
When I call to You in prayer

I can sing with my last breath
Sing for I know
That I'll sing with the angels
And the saints around the throne

Dear Lord,

I want to be stunned by You. I want to worship You.
I don't want to talk about what I need or what I don't have that I want,
I just want to praise You for what You have already provided for me.

In Jesus's Name, Amen.

Epilogue

My dearest girlfriend is Christie. If you've been around me or read much of what I've written, you've already met her. I won't rehash our entire story, but Christie and I have been best friends since our cribs were side-by-side in the Cradle Roll nursery at Hickory Grove Baptist Church in the late '60s. Wow, I can't believe I just wrote '60s. I'm gonna need a minute.

Pause.

Unpause.

When we were kids, one of our favorite make-believe activities was to play school. Little did we know that our imaginary play would one day become reality. We both graduated college with elementary education degrees. While we each started our careers teaching children, my career took a major turn in the late '90s—and an even sharper turn when I responded to God's invitation to ministry. I've never regretted my decision to leave education, and Christie has never regretted her decision to remain in education. However, there is one decision I do regret: moving my retirement money that I earned while teaching. This is a decision my bestie and I don't share—and she doesn't regret it. Let me tell you why:

In the early 1990s, when we both joined the field of teaching, our state offered an incredibly generous benefit. Teachers in the North Carolina education system would, upon retirement, receive free health insurance for the remainder of their lives, if they met two stipulations. (No one could have known at the time what an outstanding benefit this would be.) Receiving this free health insurance would be dependent upon (1) teachers being fully vested (defined as teaching at least five years) and (2) not moving our retirement money to another investment account. Can you believe that!?

As I stated, I left the education field before I was fully vested. And much to my now much older chagrin, I moved my retirement money. (I'm quite certain I heard you gasp.) On the other hand, Christie has not moved her retirement investment; therefore, it has been growing since she began teaching. The story gets better, so hang in there with me.

Christie left education to start her family three months short of her full vesting period. (You can't predict when those babies will make their way into the world.) So, the free health insurance is not available to her *unless* she goes back to teach in public education to complete her five years. But even though she's not fully vested, Christie will still receive her retirement money. However, if she returns to teach for three more months, she will receive *both* the investment money and the health insurance when she reaches retirement.

This dovetails beautifully with our four-week conversation of the 320 Life. In living the three *yes, no,* and *maybe* principles that we've studied, we receive the fullness of our eternal life while we are here on earth. Our relationship with our Savior is alive, personal, and interactive. Our spiritual waltz is danced to a beautiful symphony, and our dance card is filled as we enjoy every day with our Bridegroom in anticipation of one day seeing Him face-to-face. But what happens if we don't live these principles? What if we decide after Jesus saves us to live in spiritual mediocrity? What great questions!

Spiritual mediocrity means you make the decision to settle for less than Christ died to give you—to *not* be fully vested. You settle for less: less joy, less freedom, less love, less fulfillment, less discernment. Choosing less doesn't mean you are not saved; it means you aren't fully vested. You chose the retirement without the free health insurance.

Should Christie decide *not* to go back to public education for three months, at the age of 65 she will still retire, but she will miss the fullness of what she could enjoy had she chosen to be fully vested. Should you decide not to live by the 320 Life principles, you will not be less saved, you will just miss out on all the benefits that are associated with being fully vested—spiritually speaking—while living on earth.

Oh, dear friend . . . dear, dear friend, I beg you from the deepest part of my soul, please don't get to Heaven and meet the Savior having *not* chosen to live the immeasurably more abundant life He offers. It's so much more than salvation. It's the extra nugget in the box, the BOGO you weren't expecting at the store, the hot drink paid for by the person in front of you in the drive-through. It's the unexplainable joy in moments of obedience, the inexplicable peace in times of trouble, the undeterred power to turn away in tempting scenarios, the undeniable hope in seasons of darkness, the undoubtable wisdom in cases of uncertainty . . . and so much more; more than you can ask or imagine. Be fully vested and embrace the 320 Life. The best is yet to come. I'm living proof.

Appendix 1

LIVE IT, LEARN IT, LOVE IT

Read the Bible? The whole thing? From cover to cover? Leviticus, Numbers, and Deuteronomy? I've heard they're hard to comprehend. Do I have to read the Old Testament? Jesus wasn't even born then. What if I don't understand everything? This is an abbreviated and paraphrased version of the conversation I had with the Lord when I heard His instruction to read the entire Bible.

I grew up attending church, Sunday school, and Wednesday night Bible study every week. But the thought of reading the whole Bible intimidated me. I was consumed by two fears: not being able to understand what I read and failure to finish.

To ease my anxiety, I went to my local Christian bookstore with this thought: *If I'm going to read the whole Bible, I would like a new, fresh, unwritten-in Bible.*

I previewed various types of Bibles in an array of colors, styles, translations, and formats. It seemed like hours had passed as I checked out each option. And just when I was about to give up, I pulled the *One Year Chronological Bible* from the shelf.

The format intrigued me. Short readings. An easy-to-follow daily plan. An attractive cover. The best part to me was knowing I would read the Bible in the order the events occurred. *Yes! This is the Bible for me.*

This specific Bible caused me to fall in love with God and His Word in a way I never knew was possible. I've been reading it daily since 2008. In fact, it is from *The One Year Chronological Bible* that Read Thru the Word (my online Bible study class) and Word Up Ministries (a non-profit I started in 2019; see the back of this book for the 411) were birthed.

God opened my eyes to the truths of His Word. "Open my eyes to see the wonderful truths in your instructions" (Ps. 119:18 [NLT]). You see, I thought a Christian should be able to understand the Bible completely. And, because I didn't, I thought something must be wrong with *me*.

The truth is, God will instruct us and teach us His Word as we read it. When we don't grasp something the first time we read it, it doesn't mean we are less of a

Christian. God, in His infinite wisdom, keeps some things hidden from us until just the right time. We must be diligent in our reading the Bible and in asking God to reveal the truths He wants us to know, and to be okay with the mysteries He doesn't reveal to us. Until He does (*if* He ever does), let's keep searching and studying His Word.

In this bonus teaching, I'm excited to share with you how I've fallen in love with God's Word. We first learn it, then we live it, and then we love it.

Something to View

VIDEO LISTENING GUIDE

"All Scripture is inspired by God and is useful to teach us what is true and to make us realize what is wrong in our lives. It corrects us when we are wrong and teaches us to do what is right. God uses it to prepare and equip his people to do every good work." 2 Tim. 3:16–17 (NLT)

Scripture:

❖ is inspired by God.

❖ is useful for teaching what is true.

❖ is useful for making us realize what is wrong in our lives.

❖ corrects us when we are wrong.

❖ teaches us what is right.

If Scripture is a _____, *then* we are _____.

A learner is a disciple: student a committed _____ and _____ of Jesus Christ.

If we are learners and Scripture is our teacher, useful for helping, learning, and correcting, *then* why don't we want to learn?

We are _____.

Fear we won't .... Fear we will ....

.... them.

.... them.

"The LORD our God has secrets known to no one. We are not accountable for them, but we and our children are accountable forever for all that he has revealed to us, so that we may obey all the terms of these instructions." Deut. 29:29 (NLT)

.... them.

"I appeal to you therefore, brothers, by the mercies of God, to present your bodies as a living sacrifice, holy and acceptable to God, which is your spiritual worship. Do not be conformed to this world, but be transformed by the renewal of your mind, that by testing you may discern what is the will of God, what is good and acceptable and perfect." Rom. 12:1–2 (ESV)

"So here's what I want you to do, God helping you: Take your everyday, ordinary life—your sleeping, eating, going-to-work, and walking-around life—and place it before God as an offering. Embracing what God does for you is the best thing you can do for him. Don't become so well-adjusted to your culture that you fit into it without even thinking. Instead, fix your attention on God. You'll be changed from the inside out. Readily recognize what he wants from you, and quickly respond to it. Unlike the culture around you, always dragging you down to its level of immaturity, God brings the best out of you, develops well-formed maturity in you." Rom. 12:1–2 (THE MESSAGE)

.... them.

"Your word is a lamp to guide my feet and a light for my path." Ps. 119:105 (NLT)

As you open your heart to learn the Word, a desire to obey it will be born.

.... them.

_____ them.

"Do not merely listen to the word, and so deceive yourselves. Do what it says."

James 1:22 (NIV)

_____ to them.

"If you listen to constructive criticism, you will be at home among the wise."

Prov. 15:31 (NLT)

The natural response to learning it and living it is _____
_____.

_____ them.

"The law from your mouth is more precious to me than thousands of pieces of silver and gold." Ps. 119:72 (NIV)

_____ them (personalize them for yourself and others).

"I meditate on your precepts and consider your ways." Ps. 119:15 (NIV)

"I pray that the eyes of your [my] heart may be enlightened in order that you [I] may know the hope to which he [You] has [have] called you [me], the riches of his [Your] glorious inheritance in his holy people, and his [Your] incomparably great power for us [me, because I believe] who believe." Eph. 1:18–19 (NIV)

_____ in obedience.

"If you love me, keep my commands." John 14:15 (NIV)

Bottom line: you will never learn them, live them, or love them if you don't read them.

You will not be able to stop yourself. You will:

- experience His power more profoundly.

- sense His presence more authentically.

- know His love more deeply.

"Happy is that man who possesses a Bible! Happier still is he who reads it! Happiest of all is he who not only reads it, but obeys it, and makes it the rule of his faith and practice!"

—John Charles Ryle

Appendix 2

HIDING SCRIPTURE IN YOUR
HEART AND MIND

What genre of music did you enjoy most when you were young? When you're driving down the road, alone, and one of your favorite songs comes on the radio, do you turn the volume up and belt out every word? I have to say, I impress myself when I can easily sing lyrics I haven't heard in a decade or two. As soon as any '80s rock song starts to play, I teleport in my mind to center stage and the steering wheel becomes a drum . . . *Don't stop believin'!*

Seriously, at my age I have a hard time remembering why I walk into a room, but I can recall every word to a song I learned 40 years ago. Oh, and do you remember your childhood home telephone number? I do, and I may have recently given it to someone who asked me for my cell number. I'm quite sure I am not alone.

So, the million-dollar question is: *how can it be so easy to remember the words to our favorite songs, both past and present, yet memorizing Scripture is so difficult?* Ah, I wish I had the answer to that question, but alas, I haven't studied neuroscience or spiritual battles quite enough to deep dive into all the reasonings our memories and minds do what they do. However, I have pulled together some methods that might help us remedy this conundrum.

I've searched the entire biblical canon and have not been able to locate a verse that *commands* us to memorize Scripture. There are many verses, especially in Psalm 119, that *highly suggest* that we learn God's Word. As we learned early in this study, there are benefits to learning and memorizing Bible verses and tucking them deep in our soul and mind. Below are a few great verses that strongly encourage us to commit God's Word to memory.

"I have stored up your word in my heart, that I might not sin against you."

Ps. 119:11 (ESV)

"How shall a young man cleanse his way? By taking heed and keeping watch [on himself] according to Your word [conforming his life to it]." Ps. 119:9 (AMPC)

"Let the teaching of Christ live inside you richly. Use all wisdom to teach and counsel each other. Sing psalms, hymns, and spiritual songs with thankfulness in your hearts to God." Col. 3:16 (ERV)

VIDEO LISTENING GUIDE

Like you, I feel the tension between remembering less important things—song lyrics, old phone numbers, and useless facts about our favorite sports team—and not remembering the most important things in our life—God, Jesus, the Holy Spirit, and the Bible. So, together, let's put into practice some easy memorization methods to help us always keep the persons of the Trinity and the Word on the forefront of our mind.

1. Select a _____ of interest or need.

   Seeing immediate application of a verse will stir your desire to commit it to memory.

2. Start _____.

   A shorter verse is less intimidating than a longer one with many commas and conjunctions. Starting small will build your confidence.

3. Extend _____.

   The Bible doesn't teach anything about heavenly demerits for missing a thee, thou, or ye, nor for quoting an incorrect Scripture reference. Give yourself grace if you miss a word or can't recall the exact location of a verse.

4. Write it down and _____ to it.

   People learn in different ways. Some learn visually, some audibly, some tangibly, etc. Because of this, take time to learn in various methods. Write the verse on an index card or a sticky note (my personal favorite). Place the verse in areas you frequent so you see and read it often. Also, listen to the verse on an audio version of the Bible (you can find many translations for free on YouTube or purchase one online). Or create a craft, drawing, or decorative journaling entry of the verse to use as a tangible reminder.

5. Break and _____.

   Break large verses up into smaller sections. Write the verses on different colors of paper or different index cards, then, as you memorize them, put the pieces of the verse together.

6. Invite a _____.

   Almost everything is better when done with a friend. Accountability is a key component to success. Ask a friend or family member to memorize Scripture with you and check in on each other's progress.

7. Create a _____.

   Use a spiral index card notebook to record the verses you are learning. Keep your mini-Bible in your purse or work tote. Use one with colored paper to organize your verses by topic.

8. Study various _____.

   Some verses are easier to learn in a different translation that uses more modern language. Utilize an online website or Bible app to easily look up different translations (like Bible Hub, BibleGateway, or YouVersion).

9. _____.

   Read the same verse over and over every day for a week or a month (however long it takes you to commit it to memory). Say it out loud as you do housework. Put it to a melody you're familiar with and sing it repeatedly.

10. Know the _____.

    Read the entire book of the verse you're memorizing and study commentaries on it. In order to rightly apply Scripture to our lives, we must understand the context in which it was written. Study the author of the verse, the audience it was written to, why it was written, the culture during the time it was written, the Greek or Hebrew words, etc. The more you know about the context around the verse, the more the verse will come alive to you, and you'll understand the original and intended meaning.

"The Bible in the memory is better than the Bible in the book case."
—Charles Haddon Spurgeon

*Answers to the Something to
View Video Listening Guides*

WEEK 1: THE 320 LIFE

What the 320 Life is *not*?

- ✤ A bunch of rules.

- ✤ Getting all the **religious** things **right**.

- ✤ Working for salvation.

- ✤ The more I do, the more I'm blessed **mentality**.

What *is* the 320 Life?

- ✤ It's living **righteously** with complete **freedom** and **trust** that everything that happens is sovereignly planned, because you love God, not because you want more and more from Him.

- ✤ Greater than the sum of your:

    past **failures** and experiences.

    hopes and **accomplishments**.

    bank **accounts**.

    titles and **degrees**.

The 320 Life is complete surrender:

- ✤ to a God you can't **see**.

- ✤ to experience the **unknown** and **unexplained**.

Our spiritual wealth is found when we say:

- ❖ *yes* to God, because *yes* cultivates trust <u>in</u> God.

- ❖ *no* to self, because *no* invites revelation <u>from</u> God.

- ❖ *maybe* to others, because *maybe* welcomes freedom <u>with</u> God.

WEEK 2: THE WEALTH OF YES

The life you've always wanted and wondered how to have is found at the **intersection** of God's Word and your **obedience** to it.

The life you always wanted starts with a **yes**.

Love God with a **yes**.

Ask God for **help**.

Turn to Psalm 119:34

"Give me **understanding** and I will obey your instructions; I will put them into practice with all my heart." (NLT)

Turn to Psalm 119:73

"You made me; you created me. Now give me the **sense** to follow your commands." (NLT)

Every *yes*!

- ❖ *Yes* brings joy.

  "Joyful are people of integrity, who follow the instructions of the LORD. Joyful are those who obey his laws and search for him with all their hearts." Ps. 119:1–2 (NLT)

- ❖ *Yes* gives **freedom**.

  "I will walk in freedom, for I have devoted myself to your commandments." Ps. 119:45 (NLT)

- ❖ *Yes* gives life.

  "I will never forget your commandments, for by them you give me life."
  Ps. 119:93 (NLT)

❖ *Yes* gives strength.

> "Therefore, be careful to obey every command I am giving you today, so you may have strength to go in and take over the land you are about to enter." Deut. 11:8 (NLT)

What if God asks something that is hard for me?

> "For this is the love of God, that we keep His commandments; and His commandments are not **burdensome**." 1 John 5:3 (NASB)

Always err on the side of **obedience**.

WEEK 3: THE WEALTH OF *NO*

To gain understanding of any subject, it's helpful to have a teacher. And God has given us the best one.

"But you have received the **Holy Spirit,** and He lives within you, so you don't need anyone to **teach** you what is true. For the **Spirit** teaches you **everything** you need to know, and what He **teaches** is true—it is not a lie. So just as He has taught you, remain in fellowship with Christ." 1 John 2:27 (NLT)

Who else do I need to help me understand scripture? **No one**.

Our image was **decided** and **defined** in Genesis 12:26–27.

Believers are to live **Word** fed and **Spirit** led. The Teacher helps with both.

In God's economy, the **loser** is the winner.

Loser to winner definitions:

- ❖ **Lose**: to put out of the way entirely, abolish, put an end to, ruin, render useless.

- ❖ **Life**: the vital force that animates our body for Him.

- ❖ **Save**: properly, deliver out of danger and into safety; used principally of God rescuing believers from the penalty and power of sin—and into His provisions (safety).

The Immeasurably More Life doesn't **come** without **cost**, but it is worth the price you pay.

At this point we've got to determine that our **cravings** to know Christ have to be greater than our concern over our hurt feelings.

WEEK 4: THE WEALTH OF *MAYBE*

Relaxed, confident faith in God is developed with every **yes** and **no**.

How do I determine the right service?

Recognize:

- ❖ My **Savior's voice**. You know the voice of the one you spend time with.

- ❖ My **gifts**. You have one or maybe more gifts, and you may or may not use them.

- ❖ My **commitments**. Your people and schedule matter.

- ❖ My **limitations**. God will use your limits to grow you and His Kingdom.

Even when I rightly recognize all the above, things may still go wrong. **What-ifs** might interrupt and make me second guess my **right decision**.

Naturally, even when we are confident that making our *maybe* a *yes* is the right decision, sometimes the what-ifs can't be **avoided**.

The proper response to every what-if is the same. Make every effort to **finish well**.

- ❖ Remember your place of service is to the **Lord**.

- ❖ Even if it gets **tough**, don't stop doing good.

- ❖ Everything you do for the Lord is **worthwhile**.

- ❖ Serve with **joy**.

APPENDIX 1: LEARN IT, LIVE IT, LOVE IT

If Scripture is a **teacher**, *then* we are **learners**.

A learner is a disciple: student
a committed **learner** and **follower** of Jesus Christ

We are **afraid**.

Fear we won't **understand**. Fear we will **understand**.

Learn them.

Study them.

Compare them.

Read them.

Live them.

Spotlight them.

Yield to them.

The natural response to learning it and living it is **loving it**.

Love them.

Pray them (personalize them for yourself and others).

Respond in obedience.

APPENDIX 2: HIDING SCRIPTURE IN YOUR HEART AND MIND

1. Select a **topic** of interest or need.

2. Start **small**.

3. Extend **grace**.

4. Write it down and **listen** to it.

5. Break and **learn**.

6. Invite a **friend**.

7. Create a **mini-Bible**.

8. Study various **translations**.

9. **Repetition**.

10. Know the **context**.

About the Author

Wendy is the wife of Scott, mother of Blaire and Griffin, author, speaker, and Bible study teacher. She loves lazy Sundays watching golf with her husband, thrift-store shopping with her daughter, and watching building shows with her son.

Wendy is the author of *Jesus Everlasting: Leaning On Our Counselor, Comforter, Father and Friend, Hidden Potential: Revealing What God Can Do Through You, Wait and See: Finding Peace in God's Pauses and Plans* and the *Wait and See Participant's Guide: A Six-Session Study on Waiting Well*, as well as the *Yes, No, and Maybe: Living with the God of Immeasurably More* book, study guide, and video series. She is a contributing author to the *Real-Life Women's Devotional Bible, Encouragement for Today: Devotions for Daily Living, The Reason We Speak*, and *God's Purpose for Every Woman*. Wendy is the Founder and Executive Director of Word Up Ministries.

She leads women all over the world to life change through her in-depth online Bible studies. Down-to-earth and transparent, Wendy teaches in a way that women feel she is speaking directly to their hearts. Her messages are filled with biblical insights but sprinkled with just the right amount of humor to help her audiences see she is a real, everyday woman. Wendy inspires her audiences to:

- ❖ make spending time in God's Word each day a priority,

- ❖ look for God working around them every day, and

- ❖ view life with a God-first perspective

Connect with Wendy

🌐 wendypope.org
✉️ wendy@wendypope.org
📘 www.facebook.com/WendyPopeOfficial
🐦 @wendybpope
📷 Wendy_Pope

Word Up Ministries is a 501(c)(3) non-profit, whose purpose is to nurture and enhance the spiritual growth of Christians all over the world through the teaching of God's Word; to teach those who are not Christians about Jesus and His saving grace, so they might be saved; and to produce and distribute Biblical content through video, social media, and written formats in order to disciple and help mature the faith of every member.

We have had the privilege of leading over 5,000 men and women through the One Year Chronological Bible (NLT). We look forward to broadening the reach of God's Word through Word Up Ministries by continuing our daily teachings and exploring avenues of ministry. To discover more about or to support Word Up Ministries, visit www.wordupministries.org.

WEEK 1

1. GotQuestions.org. "What Does It Mean That God Can Do Immeasurably More Than We Can Ask or Imagine in Ephesians 3?" Accessed September 28, 2022. www.gotquestions.org/immeasurably-more.html.

2. Bible Hub, s.v. "*huper*," accessed October 16, 2022, https://biblehub.com/greek/5228.htm.

3. Bible Hub, s.v. "perissos," accessed October 16, 2022, https://biblehub.com/greek/4053.htm.

4. Wiersbe, Warren W. *The Wiersbe Bible Commentary.* Colorado Springs, CO: David C Cook, 2007.

5. Chamber, Oswald. My Utmost for His Highest. Grand Rapids, MI: Oswald Chambers Publications Association, Ltd. Discovery House, 1992.

WEEK 3

1. Clarke, Adam. "Bible Commentaries Psalms 119." Commentary on the Bible. Study Light. Nashville: Abigdon Press. Accessed September 30, 2022. www.studylight.org/commentaries/eng/acc/psalms-119.html.

2. Bible Hub, s.v. "makarion," accessed October 14, 2022, https://biblehub.com/greek/makarion_3107.htm.

3. Blue Letter Bible, s.v. "*appolymmi*," accessed October 15, 2022, https://www.blueletterbible.org/lexicon/g622/kjv/tr/0-1/.

4. Study Light, s.v. "psychế," accessed October 20, 2022, https://studylight.org/lexicons/eng/greek/5590.html.

5. Bible Hub, s.v. "sózó," accessed October 15, 2022, https://biblehub.com/greek/4982.htm.

WEEK 4

1. Keil, Carl Friedrich, and Franz Delitzsch. "Commentaries Psalm 119:45." Biblical Commentary on the Old Testament. Bible Hub. T & T Clark, 1866. Accessed October 3, 2022. https://biblehub.com/commentaries/psalms/119-45.htm.

2. Geneva Study Bible. "Commentaries Psalm 119:45." Bible Hub. Accessed October 3, 2022. https://biblehub.com/ commentaries/psalms/119-45.htm.

3. Stephen, John, quoted in Charles H. Spurgeon. The Treasury of David, Vol. VI, Psalm CXIX to CXXIV. New York: Funk & Wagnalls, 1882.

4. GotQuestions.org. "What Does it Mean that the Rocks Will Cry Out in Luke 19:40?" Accessed September 14, 2022. www.gotquestions.org/rocks-cry-out.html.

5. Tomlin, Chris. "How Can I Keep from Singing." Matt Redman and Ed Cash. Recorded 2006. Track 1 on See the Morning. Sixsteps Music/ EMI CMG Publishing, compact disc.

APPENDIX 1

1. Journey. "Don't Stop Believin'." Steve Perry, Neil Schon, and Jonathan Cain. Recorded 1981. Escape. Columbia Records.

Bible Credits

Unless otherwise noted, all Scripture quotations are taken from HOLY BIBLE, NEW INTERNATIONAL VERSION®, NIV® Copyright © 1973, 1978, 1984, 2011 by Biblica, Inc.® Used by permission. All rights reserved worldwide.

Scripture quotations marked NLT are taken from the *Holy Bible*, New Living Translation, copyright © 1996, 2004, 2015 by Tyndale House Foundation. Used by permission of Tyndale House Publishers, Inc., Carol Stream, Illinois 60188. All rights reserved.

Scripture quotations marked AMP are taken from the Amplified® Bible, copyright © 2015 by The Lockman Foundation. Used by permission. (www.Lockman.org).

Scripture quotations marked AMPC are taken from the Amplified® Bible Classic Edition, copyright © 1954, 1987 by The Lockman Foundation. Used by permission. (www.Lockman.org).

Scripture quotations marked CEV are taken from the Contemporary English Version®. Copyright © 1995 American Bible Society. All rights reserved.

Scripture quotations marked ESV are taken from the ESV® Bible (The Holy Bible, English Standard Version®), copyright © 2001 by Crossway, a publishing ministry of Good News Publishers. Used by permission. All rights reserved.

Scripture quotations marked GNT are taken from the Good News Translation® (Today's English Version, Second Edition). Copyright © 1992 American Bible Society. All rights reserved.

Scripture quotations marked KJ21 are taken from the 21st Century King James Version®, copyright © 1994. Used by permission of Deuel Enterprises, Inc., Gary, SD 57237. All rights reserved.

Scripture quotations marked or denoted as KJV or King James are taken from the King James Version of the Bible. (Public Domain.)

Scripture quotations marked NASB are taken from the New American Standard Bible®, Copyright © 1960, 1971, 1977, 1995, 2020 by The Lockman Foundation. All rights reserved. Used by permission. (www.Lockman.org).

CPSIA information can be obtained
at www.ICGtesting.com
Printed in the USA
BVHW020915010323
659463BV00001B/1